Six Ways:
Approaches & E
for Practical A.

AIDAN WACHTER

Six Ways:
Approaches & Entries for Practical Magic

Aidan Wachter

Red Temple Press
· M · M · X · V · I · I · I ·

Six Ways: Approaches & Entries for Practical Magic
by Aidan Wachter

Red Temple Press: info@redtemplepress.com
Aidan Wachter: info@aidanwachter.com

Cover and all internal illustrations by Aidan Wachter
Book design by Dr. Jenn Zahrt, www.jennzahrt.com
Copydited by Erzebet Barthold, www.erzebetbarthold.com
Written by Aidan Wachter, www.aidanwachter.com

Printed in the United States of America
First Printing: 2018
ISBN: 978-0-9993566-0-9

NOTE: Magic and sorcery, while being essential human activities, are just about as safe as the rest of the things we do in life. The author and publisher are not responsible for any adverse effects or reactions due to use, misuse, misunderstanding, and/or grievous errors in the application of the concepts and practices within. Enjoy!

ACKNOWLEDGEMENTS

Books are not written in a vacuum. This one came about due to prodding by the fabulous clients of my talismanic jewelry work. I ended up writing it to have a single place to refer people to who had questions about what I do. I foolishly thought it would be "easier" to "just" write a book! This is that book.

Eternal thanks to my wife Blu, without whom this book would not exist.

Much appreciation and deep, deep thanks to the first readers for their invaluable feedback: Fabeku Fatunmise, Briana Saussy, Dre Achilleus, Jonathan Emmett, and William Jones. Fabeku and Dre in particular helped to shape the text in numerous ways that made it clearer and more reflective of my intentions.

To Erzebet Barthold for copyediting.
To Dr. Jenn Zahrt for layout, design, and index.

Written with extensive assistance and input from the Shop Fairies.
All the errors are mine.

CONTENTS

PRETEXT

I wrote *Six Ways* to fill a gap that as far as I am aware, hasn't been filled quite to my liking. This gap is the space between a simple, direct, non-dogmatic and internally consistent magical approach and its application in the modern world. I've seen and read a lot of spell books, a lot of theory books, a lot of historical texts, a lot of pagan reconstructions, a lot of books on magical "tech," and a lot of what are primarily expressions of religious ritual practices. These are all fine things, and I have a small selection of each type of book in my collection. That said, the majority of magical books I have come across are of two types. The first is not practical enough, meaning they don't really provide a clear enough context to allow someone to take the practices provided and really run with them. The second type is actually *too* context driven, as in a text on traditional witchcraft, or a ceremonial grimoire for example, where it is often assumed that you adhere to a particular set of beliefs, philosophies, and aesthetics. If, however, you do not, they may not be of much use at all beyond their value as literature.[1] In *Six Ways* I am attempting to do a few things. The first is to share how I actually think about and experience the work that I do, as well as how it fits within my life overall. This piece is to me the missing link in a lot of magical writing. Having the technical bits (the "how to" portion) without the internal reasoning or application within the larger milieu of a life tends to limit the usefulness of the information. The second bit relates to the technical skills I use (and the steps I took or now suggest to develop them as skills) shown in such a way that the reader is not locked into the specific methodology I use. The third piece is focused on developing or remembering the sorcerous worldview, and is a collection of windows and doors (the approaches and entries of the subtitle of the book) that one can

---

1   "Their value as literature," however should not be discounted! Viewing magical texts primarily as literature is actually a really fine approach that I never even considered until a few years ago.

use to access these states of being. The last and most important piece of the book covers a whole lot of my thinking and feeling behind what it has taken for me to make, maintain, and deepen contact with the Otherworld and the spirits of the Field,[2] and how another might go about such a task.

Six Ways came about via a rather twisty path. Through my practice of sorcery and magic, I came to know a symbolic jeweler, my late friend Mark Defrates, in New Orleans in the early 1990's. Along with Mark's wife Pamela Daley, we in time generated an international chaos magic group known as the (Z) Cluster. In the late nineties, I learned the basics of silver and gold smithing from Mark, and in 2012, I decided to try my hand at being a talismanic jeweler as a full-on trade. When I first began offering my talismanic jewelry for sale, I expected my client base to be largely composed of "lifer" magicians, witches and sorcerers. This turned out to be half true! The other half turned out to be people who recognized that there was "something to this magic thing" and who may have had a practice of sorts, but had not dedicated their lives to the study of magic or occultism. Primarily for this second half I began to write blog posts, mostly to answer repeated questions about how I did what I did, what I thought about it, and how others might approach similar types of work.

Surprisingly to me, I began to get a large amount of feedback from people who actually were magical "lifers" that what I was writing was helpful to them as well. From all of this feedback, *Six Ways* was born.

I have written, to the best of my ability, what is intended to be as close to a stand-alone text as possible.[3] I have done this for the folks who are not interested in dedicating themselves to years (or a life) of occult study but are seeking a direct pathway to entering, developing, and deepening their magical practices. At the same time, I have attempted to share the absolutely most useful pieces and views I have found along my path, which I hope will serve the lifers as well! We shall see in time if I have succeeded.

May the Spirits of the Field bless you and your works!

---

2   The Field is the term I use for the whole of the known and unknown universe and its visible and invisible inhabitants and structure. The Field is the totality of manifest and unmanifest reality. Sorcery is the art of effective inter-being with the Field.

3   There is a small suggested reading list at the back of the book for those interested in diving deeper.

CHAPTER ONE

INTRODUCTION

This book is about sorcery and magic,[1] as I know and work it. Magic and sorcery have many definitions, and will have many more as we move as a species forward through time. The basic idea is that there are ways of being and interacting in the world that allow for certain kinds of communication, the production of change on both internal and external levels, and the development of what could be called "special skills and talents."

These are psychic powers or arts, in the old usage of the word: meaning "relative to the soul, spirit, mind." These arts of soul, spirit, and mind come down to us in various ways. They come as full-blown systems of magic or witchcraft, as religious practices, as shamanry,[2] as tales and ideas surviving via folklore, song, poetry and literature.

My approach is this: what works, works. That which does not work, or whose costs outweigh their benefits, should be discarded or modified until the balance skews more favorably. This is a trial and error process, and there's no way to avoid that aspect from what I've seen.

For myself, magic is not a religious practice. It deals with a number (a great, unknowable number) of internal and external players. Spirits, Powers, and Others are the terms I use and prefer, while others may feel the need to get more specific as to the particular natures of these beings.

Magic and sorcery are ways of being in the world. They are ways of interacting and inter-being with the world itself and its visible and invisible structures and inhabitants, which all together I refer to as the Field. The aim of magic as I know it is to increase the quantity and quality of usable and useful information, communication, options, and avenues of change

---

1 Magic and sorcery are used interchangeably throughout this book. The only real difference between them that I can see is that when you tell someone you practice sorcery, they don't usually ask you to show them a trick.

2 Shamanry is a convention that makes sense to me, which I learned of via Marcus R. McCoy.

and movement within our selves and our worlds. It is an art of total responsibility, careful attention, and reciprocity. Lately I've been defining magic as the art of falling in love with the Field and its inhabitants.

There is little "new" here if such a thing can even exist in a what appears to be hundreds of thousand years of continuous human practice. There are ideas here whose roots are in chaos magick, self-hypnosis, fortune telling, shamanry, witchcraft, ritual magic, Wicca, hoodoo, folk magic, and less reputable sources.

My interest has always been guided by my own internal logic. An idea has to clearly make some kind of sense for me to really dig into it. I've never been good at the whole "do this even though it makes no sense, it'll make sense later" approach. It also has been shown that my internal logic isn't all that logical to many other people!

Included are a number of exercises and approaches. They are the pieces that I have found most useful in the long term. Many things are good fun for a short stint, fewer are worth shacking up with, and even less are worth marrying. These are the marriage-worthy practices and viewpoints as I have found them and come to know them in close relationship.

In some cases, I can tell you where the particular approach came from, but in many more, they have been modified over extended time frames and may bear little resemblance to their original forms, and may have diverged so far from the original intention as to be different things entirely.

These magical techniques and ideas will only be helpful in actual practice. If you do not actually do the work little will come from it. At the same time, they are not dogma. If something here makes sense for you to work with, you will likely have to adapt it to your own unique self, to your specific context and needs.

I believe that these concepts of "approaches and entries" are important. Experience has shown that I can't really teach anyone to do what I do. However, it can be very helpful (for me at least) to get a window into another's approach. If I can find a workable approach, however imperfect it may be, if it allows me to see how a process works in practice, then I can replicate the type of work shown in myriad, personally appropriate ways. If I can find an entry, a door into a space or practice, in most cases that is the hard part. Once I have access into the house, so to speak, I am free to explore.

CHAPTER TWO

INTENTION

Most forms of magic and sorcery (and really most actions at all!) work best with some kind of an intention. So here is mine for this book:

> *I write this book as a gift to the Spirits of the Field and as an aid to those who seek to know and work with them.*

If you wish to dive right into the action part of the book, try this for an entry:

Take a piece of paper and a pen and write out why you are reading this book. Narrow it down to a single, clear sentence. This may be rather hard! As arts of communication, magic and sorcery benefit from clarity. Often this means starting from a wide view, a very general stance, but one that is "true to you." Here are some helper questions.

> *What are you seeking in your life generally?*
> *What are you seeking to learn or gain from the practice of magic?*
> *What blocks your motion in the directions you desire to move?*
> *What aids you?*
> *What hinders you right now, at this very moment?*
> *What do you love in this very moment?*

These types of questions can help in tightening up a magical intention.

Now take your intention (and it's OK if it's more than one sentence, just don't get too epic), and write it out again on a small square of paper, perhaps three inches across. Read your intention aloud three times, kiss the paper three times, and breathe onto it three times, and say:

> *As it was*
> *As it is*
> *As it shall be*[1]

---

1 Threes are important to me, and to a number of streams of magic. For works of change,

Fold the paper in half, folding it towards you, and place it in the back of this book.

Sorcery is the art of communication with the Field and its inhabitants. The Field is highly responsive to our intentions, both those stated and unspoken. Magic is primarily learning and remembering how to clarify both the known and unknown intentions (or desires, if that language works better for you) that fill us and how to "speak" them to the Field in a way that increases the possibility of a positive, helpful response.

This is how I approach it.

---

try using three repetitions, elements, words, components, what have you. Likewise, sets of four lend themselves to keeping things as they are.

down into myself the ability to perceive my blind spots in a situation, who am I to say that it is not a spirit who responds and lends me its vision?

In this concrete and concretized world it is easy to think that what I know, what I see, and what I experience is clearly true and accurate, or else clearly false and inaccurate. But there are vast shaping influences on both myself as perceiver, as knower, as well as on the data stream whatever its form or source.

In magical practice, perception changes and shifts. If I am open-minded enough to try new approaches (without being so open-minded my brain falls out, as the saying goes) in an inquisitive and explorative fashion, I can find new-to-me ways of being and doing that which I have decided or discovered needs to be done.

The root value in this shifting of perceptions is the possibility of discovering new and different options. I can use various schools of knowledge to help with this. When I first decided to see if I could move my consciousness or sense of self, which I had been culturally indoctrinated to believe resided in my brain, I first had to be open to the possibility that perhaps this was not a hard fact. I learned that in earlier times and cultures, the self or soul was believed to reside in the heart and at other times, the liver. So just based on these once known "facts" it seemed I should surely be able to move my sense of self between these three locations. I also found that there were schools of thought where the soul or self is mobile, that it can leave the body entirely, so that was at least possible as well. I was not required to believe these things were objectively true, they were simply tools to let me see that what I "knew" to be true based upon my cultural training and education was quite possibly less than true, or perhaps just "not always true" or "not exclusively true."

Here is an experiment you can try if you'd like to play with these things.

Let's decide to work with something generally useful. Let's also decide that this is the quality of being able to see more available options than is usual. These are forms of magical works usually called "Road Openers."

So this then might be our stated focus: "greater awareness of beneficial options available to me now."

We can write an evocation (calling up) for it, which might go something like this:

Here and now, in this place, I call upon the powers of Optionality!
Come before me now, and let me see your nature!
Come before me now, and speak[2] to me of possibilities, of outcomes benefi-
    cial to me, that I have been unable to see.
Be present, here and now, and aid me in my work.
Show me the roads open to me.
Show me the doors that have been hidden from me.
Give me the keys to open those hidden doors.
Give me the ability to discern the paths available to me, both obvious and
    obscured, and to choose among them wisely.

Or I could perform an invocation (calling into) instead:

Here and now, in this place, I call upon the powers of Optionality!
Come into me now, and let me share in your nature!
Come into me now, that I may know the possibilities, the outcomes benefi-
    cial to me, that I have been unable to see.
Come into me now, that you may guide my hands and eyes in this work.
I see through your eyes the roads open before me.
I see the doors that were hidden from me.
I hold the keys to open those doors.
I clearly perceive the paths available to me, the obvious and the obscure,
    and I choose among them wisely.

I could sigilize the intention (see chapter 18), or create a petition for it (see chapter 17), either or both of which could be used in an invocation or evocation. I could use the intention, sigil, or petition for a candle spell (see chapter 25). I could take them into the Dreaming (see chapter 28). I could carry them into trance or meditation (see chapters 10 and 11), or bring them to the pendulum (chapter 13) for further inquiry.

All of these methods are viable, all of them can work. They can be used singly or in combination. And I still haven't really addressed that question of spirit, God, deity or quality, have I? Perhaps it isn't all that important to have that answer right now anyway. Perhaps I will choose one answer now, and another later, if and when it makes sense to do so.

---

2   In this sense, "speak" and "show" are shorthand for "make me aware of in some way."

The process of magic of any kind involves picking a focus or direction (what I wish to do, or where or who I wish to be, what spirit or type of spirit I wish to contact or commune with, what kind of influences I wish to call to me or to send outward) and setting out in that direction, working to create changes that bring me closer to that thing (or vice versa), or which causes that change in my world. So I could say that sorcery is a decision-based art. From this point of view, there are many methods, practices, and tools I may find useful to help with the decision-making process. If I read cards, what I learn from them may help me to decide on a course of action. If I meditate I may gain clarity on my motivations for wanting to change or become aware of the need to address something that blocks or distracts me. If I interact with a spirit I may be given information (and homework!) that helps me to know what I can do to achieve my aims.

Along these lines, sitting in meditation one day, I had the realization that I made many of the same decisions over and over, day after day, perhaps even hour by hour. This added up to a lot of decisions! So I began to search for ways to make my life easier. What I came up with still sounds stupid when I say it, but it worked absolute wonders.

My revelation was this: I can decide to decide something once if I so choose. I am not obligated to revisit my decisions. That my discursive mind would prefer to loop back and second guess things and turn them over to see if their bottoms have changed in some new and fascinating way doesn't mean I have to pay any attention to it. This takes practice to actually pull off. There were some conversations I had to have with my mind and my selves about it.

If you would like to try this, I suggest starting with nonsense things. Eliminate a habit and replace it with another, something of very limited emotional/psychic loading. Treat your change as a deeply ingrained habit of huge importance. I remember deciding to stir my coffee counter-clockwise. I decided that nickels were evil and must not be touched, and that dimes were sacred and must be hoarded! I decided that I really truly needed to put on my shoes in the reverse order. I did all of these things.

Whatever you decide to change, if you decide to try this, the important part is how you talk to yourself and others about it after the fact. When your mind tells you that it's all right to have just this one nickel, you reply "I decided nickels were evil and I would not touch them. It is done." When you find one in your pocket? Drop it like a hot rock! The same for when you realize you put on your left shoe first. This is important! You take it off and put the right one on! Why? Because you decided to. Why did you decide to? Because you fucking made a choice. It's done.

Once you get the basics down on fairly meaningless things, you can begin to move onto subjects that matter more and are likely harder. You no longer get up early to make offerings to the spirits before work because you should, or because that's the right thing to do. You do it because you decided to, and it's just fucking done. This can extend out to all areas of your life.

Sorcery is not strictly about bringing into our world what we would like to have in it. It's equally about weeding out that which does not serve us as well. We live in a time of choice overload. Most of these choices barely deserve the name. We can free up a huge amount of bandwidth and reduce the noise floor (which makes room for a stronger, clearer signal) in our lives by learning to make choices and stick to them without constantly revisiting and renegotiating them.

This combined approach is how I learned to do effective magic. I learned to use all of my skills, meditation, trance, ritual, sigils and petitions, discernment, self-knowledge, knowledge of others, self-care and protection work and I began to clear out all that was "not of my life as I wished it to be." I then began to use all of my skills to draw to me what I desired instead. The work of one side supports the other.

How this seems to work is that we create a vacuum by shedding that which no longer serves us while working to fill it with something that does. Over and over, day after day and year after year, this process of clearing out what we do not want in our lives and replacing it with something which moves us closer to what we really do want is to me the very heart of practical sorcery.

CHAPTER FOUR

ANIMISM, ESSENCE, SYMBIOSIS

The basic framework or worldview I find the most useful and accurate is a form of animism. Animism is:

~ A belief that spirits inhabit or indwell some or all classes of natural objects, locations, and phenomena.
~ A belief that an immaterial force (or forces) animates the universe.

In the Western, industrialized world, we primarily operate culturally on a philosophic/religious base of materialism. "Materialism is a form of philosophical monism which holds that matter is the fundamental substance in nature, and that all phenomena, including mental phenomena and consciousness, are results of material interactions. Materialism is closely related to physicalism, the view that all that exists is ultimately physical."[1] From a magical perspective, this is a particularly unhelpful philosophy. Materialism limits possibilities. It inhibits the development of alternate strategies to the problems I face as a human spirit being. This does not help me to achieve my desires via magical means.

So instead of materialism, I suggest a return to animism as a model, wherein everything we come across contains at the very least the potential for sentience and agency. This means that while *I* may not have the answer to a question or the key to unlock a puzzle or open a door, *something* I could interact with, communicate with, and work with quite possibly does. And that is useful indeed.

This perception of being a part of a vast living universe of spirit-beings, be they human, animal, wind, rain, rock, or spirit-spirits produces a much larger field of options for me to work with.

This animist worldview also appears to be the (or at least "a") human

---

1   From Wikipedia, just to offend the snobs. https://en.wikipedia.org/wiki/Materialism

norm. How this might look in practice could be something like this:

The animist wakes up in the morning, and makes note of the dream she just had. She looks at the events that happened in the Dreaming, and sees that there are some potential issues at play among the spirits that dwell in and around her house. She gets up, and makes coffee. She thanks the coffee for its tasty goodness, and the water for keeping her and the rest of the world alive. She talks a bit to the cat, and thanks the dogs for watching over her and the house during the night. When the coffee is finally done, she pours two cups, one larger and one smaller. To the smaller cup, she adds cinnamon, sugar and a touch of red pepper. She also pours cold water into a small bowl, to which she adds a few pinches of dried rose petals. She takes the smaller cup of coffee into the living room and places it on the mantle in front a turtle shell and a few stones. She speaks: *"Spirits and allies who aid and guard me, I give thanks to you. I ask that you bless all who dwell in this house, and all the creatures with whom I share this land. Watch over all of us, and guide us to make the best use of our intentions, time, and energy. I thank you. May there be peace between us always."* The animist then takes the bowl with the water and rose petals out the front door, through the yard, and out to the gate that leads to the street. Just inside the gate, she places the bowl of water on the ground, dipping her fingers into the bowl, and traces a sign upon the gate itself. She says: *"Creature of iron, of discretion and discernment, I make this offering to you. May you be ever blessed for the work that you do, and may you always stand strong against those who would do us harm. Keep out all who wish us ill, and only allow those who bring love and kindness to enter this space."* She checks the lock on the gate, and returns inside the house to finish her own coffee.

The animist lives in a spirit-filled and spirit-infused world. She lives in a house, and the house itself lives and has a spirit. She "has a" cat and dogs, but they also have lives and spirits of their own. House, cat, dogs, woman, land, water, coffee, and gate are all beings, each with its own nature, who all choose to live together and in a sense work together towards common goals. All of them together can be thought of as joining together into another, larger being.[2]

2   The kind of animism I suggest is not necessarily a completely true and accurate description of reality. All that is required initially is to accept that it might possibly be true and act accordingly. In time it may be proven "true enough" to be useful.

Let's take another look at this spirit-animism as it relates to magic.

I perceive myself as a human-spirit-being dwelling among other spirit-beings. The most obvious of these other beings are my wife, my dogs, the cat, the ducks brooding in the bathroom, and the chickens sleeping in the trees outside my window. There are also entire other ranges of beings I know are about, but am a bit less aware of: the moths and other flying insects, the mice, rats, rabbits, ravens, hawks, snakes, lizards, on and on. These form part of the animal side of the immediate "world" that my house sits in. But there is more still: the insects in the soil, all the various plant life all around me, the mites that live on my skin, the bacteria in my gut, in the soil, and the bacteria I cultivate in my fermented foods, growing happily on top of the refrigerator.

Imagine, if you will, that every one of these things was/is a being more or less like you or me. Many are playing similar games, trying to get lucky in love, trying to survive the night, hunting for food.

Now add to that: the trees are their own family. The cholla (a type of cactus), junipers, and piñon pines all work together to do whatever it is they are doing. The rabbits and rodents assist (via help or harm) and the snakes do as well.

I, like all flesh-creatures, am not simply host to a vast array of beings – bacteria, viruses, mitochondria, blood cells, bone cells, genes – I am the world they create. I am filled with legions.

Animism suggests that we are equally surrounded and enfolded by spirit-beings. The individual and clan-spirits of the rabbits, the pack rats and the snakes all have a stake in things. As do the dead of the land, the faerie hosts, all the invisible people, the Others. The land spirit itself. Add in the wind, the rain, and the sky spirits.

In my biological animist view, we are all cells within the vast body that is the Field. We hunt in order to eat, or simply because hunting is our nature. Some cells gather together to aid one another, some to cast each other out or destroy each other. Some cells are mutations, diseases, dysfunctions, and need to be purged if the larger being is to thrive.

As I am only nominally aware of most of the physical life in and around me, I tend to be even less aware of the spirit ecologies I live in and move through. I am suffering from a huge disability in my ability to sense them. So it is for most of us.

To put it differently, I am limited in that I mostly tend to notice and be aware of the beings that are the most clearly like me structurally. Which means I perceive human and other animal beings more clearly than I perceive tree beings or grass beings or rock beings. It's very unusual for me to perceive beings that don't have any body that I can see, hear, smell, taste or touch. However, that doesn't mean they aren't there, just that I have limited perceptual abilities.

It is quite possible that in time I could learn to perceive these beings (via trance, meditation, divination) and it is also possible that they (the spirits or Others) don't have the same perceptual weaknesses that I have. What I mean by that is while I may not know much about them, they may know quite a bit about me. This often seems to be the case in practice.

So step one in beginning spirit work for me was admitting that I had some perceptual limitations. Moving beyond this limitation was foundational for me. Many of the practices described in this book are ways I found helpful for doing just that, to whatever degree that I have been successful.

My essential perspective is as follows. We humans are components of a vast system of sentience. This goes beyond the normal concept of living nature to include various Powers and beings, from the spirits of Fire and Earth to spirits of animals and landscape, to the personal and more general Dead to things that present as more traditionally demonic (troubling, threatening, disturbing, and scary) or angelic (helpful, protective, disturbing, and scary). In other words, beings that if "alive" are alive in a different way than you or I or the cat seem to be. For most of human existence, it appears that we have interfaced with these Others as a matter of course.

In addition to this, it seems that the Field itself is responsive and reactive to communication that it receives from the spirits that dwell in it, human or Other.

I believe that magic is something humans do and probably always have done. In the recent past, at least in the West, we have largely moved magic and sorcery into a subset of religion, orthodox or heretical, depending on the context of those involved. My personal belief is that this is an inversion. I believe that religion is an offshoot of sorcery and that sorcery (and the animism that underlies it) is the probable root of all human culture.

SYMBIOSIS

Symbiosis is a relationship of mutual benefit, a relationship between disparate species that benefits both parties. One goal I see of working in an animistic magical view is the building of symbiotic relationships with the world and spirits around us.

This is an important viewpoint to hold when working within a spirit ecosystem. I feel that most of the focus should be on creating a "happy and healthy place" that provides support and nourishment to all of the beings that are inherently interested in working inside such a relationship. The end result then is a committed "house" made up of us, the spirits that surround us, the physical areas we live and work in and their inhabitants. The entire "house" is then ideally pointed in the same direction, becoming in a sense a strong and healthy ship, with all components working together to achieve our goals. When this happens, the labor of moving forward is reduced.

I mostly sense this "strong and happy ship" as a reduction of friction. The current is with us, the winds drive our ship forward in a mostly smooth fashion. There are still hiccups and storms to weather, but things are generally moving forward in the direction we (myself and the spirits engaged in the work with me) desire them to.

The greatest tools I have to build such a spirit ecology are devotion, discretion, integrity, and consistency in action.

Devotion in action is to focus (devotion means to make primary or "first") on that which is the most important to me. Discretion in action is the ability and willingness to make intelligent decisions. Integrity in action means doing what I say I will do, and doing it to the best of my ability. Consistency in action means I strive to do all of these things all of the time.

To work in this fashion I continuously refine my focus and intentions, the direction I am heading, and take care of the company I keep, who are in a sense the crew of my ship. This also means not letting just anyone come on board. There are spirits that would be happy to move into my ship and enjoy the ride while working against my intentions, just as there are "friends" who will sleep on my couch and eat all my food if I let them, all the while trying to screw my girl behind my back. These types must go, or be brought into the program. I also have to do the same work with my own thought forms (i.e., keep the self-hater[3] in check and keep the discursive mind from playing shitty loops), and keep these processes going all of the time.

If this sounds like a lot of work, it is.[4] But the benefits from not fucking around are huge for me.

So I make offerings, and I am clear on who they are going to: those that aid and guard me, those spirits naturally occurring in the spaces I inhabit, as well as those who might block me for any reason but who are willing to cease and desist for a small fee (i.e., a seat at the offering table).

I create protective structures that work like antibodies to clear illness or disease that might otherwise infect our house.

I reiterate my intentions, through speech, sigils, petitions, vessels, talismans, ritual, or other types of magical focal points, keeping my mind clear and focused.

All of these pieces work together to create a healthy ecosystem that by its very nature supports me and those who work with me. This type of coherent multi-level approach has proven to be far more effective than a more scattered, haphazard one.

3   The Self-hater is a term I learned from Starhawk, and is a term that is pretty clear to most people, although it is perhaps not an entirely accurate title. This is a sort of internal abuser/dominator self, that seems to exist to drag us down and limit our options. It appears to be a cultural artifact, mostly present in the West.

4   But mostly in the set up phase. Once things are up and running in this fashion, it becomes if anything far less work to maintain than any other approach I have ever tried.

CHAPTER FIVE

TWO WORLDS AND IN-BETWEEN

In a view borrowed from shamanry, which is more usually called shamanism, I consider that the experienced world can be divided along two
primary lines. The first can be considered "ordinary reality." This is the
mundane world I wander through in my body, and where things like the
material existence of things seems certain. The second is "non-ordinary
reality," where a vast array of possibilities, experiences, realms and beings
exist that are not generally present (or not generally noticed) in ordinary
reality.

Some magical techniques can be fully worked in ordinary reality, like
dressing a candle, making an offering, or producing a petition or sigil. I do
ritual work physically in ordinary reality. I can build a wooden fetish[1] in
ordinary reality.

Some aspects of the work are only truly viable in non-ordinary reality,
like astral travel or shamanic journeying. In some ways, the difference between the two worlds is more of a matter of degree than a hard wall. When
I am carving a fetish, I can move between the two. In ordinary reality, I
hold the wood and the knife and sing the piece into form with hand and
voice. At the same time, I am singing *into* non-ordinary reality to contact
the spirits, be they the spirits that might aid me in my work, the spirits
I would like to not block or interfere with what I am doing, or the spirit
which I seek to have indwell in the fetish.

The non-ordinary reality is still reality. This is important to remember
(and can be dangerously easy to forget). It isn't the same as ordinary reality, but it is magically at least its equal.

My take on how all this sorcery stuff works is that nothing substantial
happens without access to non-ordinary reality. This need not be full-
blown trance, but in some small way my consciousness has to shift to con-

---

1   A fetish is something which is believed to possess, contain, or cause spiritual or magi-
     cal powers; an amulet or a talisman.

tact this "other world." Meditation, trance, drugs, drumming and the like can all help to facilitate this, as can firelight or candlelight and a conscious acknowledgment that I am trying to do this thing.[2] This is referenced in some ritual work where words are said along the lines of *"this space is beyond time, beyond place, is a space between the worlds,"* or in the concept of liminal (meaning threshold) spaces. Much of ritual work is the application of various methods and tools to allow this shift between worlds to occur. Magically ritual isn't so much done for the theater of telling a specific story (as it often is in religious practices) as it is using the ritual work to shift consciousness into non-ordinary reality.

Trance and journeying are the easiest (non-drug) direct roads into non-ordinary reality. And much as in India physical yoga was a preparation for the other branches of that art, meditation and other forms of "head cleaning" are preparations for accessing non-ordinary reality.

I find that having this non-ordinary reality idea in mind while I work, even at times when I don't feel that I have much access to it, still helps my efforts greatly.

To go somewhere, you have to leave where you are. Many view this traveling as "always fun," regardless of destination. Others view this as "always a little scary or uncomfortable," also regardless of destination! There are many shades in between these views. Wherever you find yourself on that spectrum, you still leave somewhere to go somewhere else.

To work towards this kind of "travel," begin to court the in-betweenness of things. Find it where you can, and begin to allow it to enchant you. In the bath, walking, in those points between waking and dreaming, notice those spaces, those little gaps, those edges where things feel a bit different, a bit odd. This is a bodily thing rather than a mind thing, this feeling.

Try this exercise out if you feel you need help to get started, and as always, modify it to suit you and your situation. As I will repeat endlessly: Context is King.

Begin to collect images, items, music, smells, etc., that all speak to you of magical Otherworlds. These can be rooted in a particular tradition or

---

2 "Do this thing" as in shift my consciousness to allow for better access to the Others.

culture, or be purely made of your own devising. You are after gut feeling rather than any kind of logic. This need not be a collection of any particular size – a few images, a few items. Add to this a candle and some incense. Bring some nice paper and pens or paints, or wood and a knife, clay, yarn, whatever art or craft tools you desire. Let your gut drive this exercise. For more than a year my ritual space was dripping in purple and orange when I was working this part! See if you can create a working space that is to your gut and heart a vision of magic. Logic and reason need not apply for this task. You may need cloth to cover things that don't fit into your vision; feel free to build what is essentially a child's secret pirate clubhouse or blanket fort to work in (remembering as always that candles start fires) that simply says to you: magic.

One night, during the early days of the waxing moon, and preferably after your usual bedtime, set this place up for your working. Make sure you can work undisturbed. I suggest having all of the bits ready, but nothing arranged in place beforehand. Let the entire process be ritual, from covering the TV and the windows to assembling your altar with the images that call you into the Otherworld. Have your music, if you use it, set up to not require attention for a few hours.

Begin to build a shrine-space to the In-between, to Magic Itself. Sing it into being, or whisper it if you do not sing. Talk to the space about your intentions. Here is an example that I have used:

> I cover the world that was and set it aside.
> I create the world that is that I may inhabit it fully.
> I build a bridge into the Otherworld,
> a place between Awake and Dreaming,
> a place between Matter and Spirit,
> a place between what was and what is and what is to come

Continue in your own words, letting the gut and heart guide your voice, your language. Try to speak or sing this in-between place into being.

As you feel connected to the Otherworld, begin to make. Use your paper, your pens, your wood or your wool, and generate a bridge to this feeling-space. Tell this creation what it is for – a physical manifestation of your contact with the Otherworld. Tell it why you are making it, why you love it. Spend as much time as seems good to you working in this space, or until you lose the thread of the feeling.

You now have one or more bridges to this feeling space. You can use them in your work as reminders that what you seek is a depth of feeling rather than the logic and reason of ordinary reality. You can use them to guide you back into the Other. This is an art, not a science.

Long-term work in what are called liminal (which means pertaining to a threshold) spaces, meaning spaces in-between worlds, forms lasting bonds between ourselves, the Otherworld and the Spirits.

I refer to it as a courtship as it is a long-term process, a long game.[3] It requires self-enchantment to awaken sensory abilities that are dormant in most of us. Find a way to fall in love with the process. Find a road in, be it trance, drumming, shamanic journeying, and dedicate yourself to its practice, to learning its ways. I am mainly a trance guy, and I'll give more specific information about that later in the book.

At some point, there is a decision to be made. At some point, there is a fork in the road that is devotion on one side and dalliance on the other. This is easy for some, and brutally hard for others. If we choose to not accept the Otherworld, the non-ordinary reality, as true, as valid, and as deserving commitment and honesty in our dealings, we will only get so far. I did some time in this kind of inconclusive space.

I see this mainly in practitioners[4] who won't relinquish the "out" of objectivity. Those who wish to argue that "ultimately nothing is true." I can only say this: you will get what you pay for, here as elsewhere. Your behavior in non-ordinary reality and in magic and sorcery in general will carry the weight you honestly give it. It will be easy to find people who will tell you otherwise, who also choose to walk the road with one foot. You get what you give.

This is not to be taken as "magic and the non-ordinary reality must become your whole life" which can (and does, and did for me) present myriad difficulties. But I realized that there was a point of diminishing

---

3   I have also found that simply accepting the long-term nature of the process seems to produce greater effects more rapidly than trying to rush it. Sorry about that, impatience!

4   A practitioner in this sense is "someone who practices magic."

returns that comes from half-assing the work I did, and the easiest way to ensure this was to not take it seriously enough. And understand this is not "serious" as in grim and without a sense of play, not at all. I mean serious instead as meaningful, not-deceitful, earnest. This has been in some way behind many of the cases where magic has turned and bit me in the ass! If I am respectful, operate with integrity (do what I say, say what I mean), and accept full responsibility for myself magically, things simply work differently. There are Spirits that won't give me the time of day otherwise, just as there are people who won't.

This devotion is at the base a commitment I have made to myself. I can of course choose to hide behind light engagement, sarcasm or objectivity (if such a thing really exists) to a degree. But all of these tools, while they may provide a sense of control, do so by creating distance. This distance is decidedly counter to the art of magic. I can't inhabit the Otherworld, non-ordinary reality, or any other aspect of my life from a distance. When I try to create such distance I opt out of a certain level of interaction with my selves (plural), with the Otherworld and with the Others.

These two worlds, ordinary and non-ordinary, the physical world and the Otherworld, are in a sense the very Theater of Magic, itself. The spaces in-between where they meet and mate, breeding magical children, are (and thus are we) the Crossroads. It is here where all we do is born, in the twilight world of ur-sorcery, the very substance of the Field.

CHAPTER SIX

GUT AND BONE

There is an interesting perceptual disconnect that comes up for me in conversation with clients that I sometimes sense right away but other times can take me awhile to recognize. It has to do with thinking and feeling as it relates to magic. I view thinking and feeling as head[1] and gut-or-bone information respectively. Both have their places, and neither will serve in each other's place very well.

I use my head and its logic to decide on a course of action. I use my gut to execute the actual magical work or to feel the truth of my oracular visioning. Our heads cannot really operate well in the slightly to completely altered states that make magic the most effective. I expect this is a modern Western issue. We have hardened the edges between us and the Other, at least in our minds. Our bodies still know better.

For instance, when trying to decide on a talismanic object (where this usually comes up with my clients), or between a few symbols, herbs, or other *materia*, we can use the head to narrow the field of options. But we must use the gut, the physicality of bone-feeling to choose what is the best option magically. This allows for a much greater influence from the Other side of things. When we see someone operating smoothly at most any art, it seems to me that this is when they have learned to set aside the head (at the appropriate time) and let the gut and bones do their thing. The head can guide, but the body does the work. Using the gut-bone information to choose means we have already committed to the work.

As long as the head is in control, I am hedging against this commitment, which means I am one-foot-in at most. I have to cross that line fully to do my best work.

If you are not sure of how to tap into this gut-bone feeling, try this. Is there a food you love? Go and find it in the store, and bring it home. At the same time, buy some of the food you most hate. Place them both on a

---

1   "Head" in this context is the "normal" logical thinking state of perception.

table in front of you, and sit with them. Seriously consider eating both of them, each in turn. You may have to really do it, you may need to eat some of your food-nemesis! Now notice: what is the difference in your body? In my case, if I seriously consider eating a raw red onion, my stomach turns, and my head tries to turn away. My body clenches, striving to create distance. My mouth tightens up and dries up. However, if the other food is something I love, say a piece of really excellent chocolate or some bacon, the reverse happens. I lean in. I can *feel* how good it will be! One is calling to me, drawing me in viscerally, as much as the other is driving me away.

Begin to bring this attention to other things. How does it feel in your body when someone is good to you, or when someone treats you poorly? Not how you are responding emotionally, but physically.[2] When you have a choice to make between two or more things, can you start to feel in your bones which one calls to you the most? This process is one many of us have unlearned, as part of life is about learning to do things we don't want to, but that we need to or are told we must. In time this can block us from fully noticing when our body, our guts, give us real, usable information.

Our bones know the way of things. Our guts understand what baffles the mind. The soul or spirit is often most clearly manifest in the sensations and language of the body. We feel called towards or driven away by people, places, and things at the gut/bone level. The head can then clarify or obscure this information, or choose to work with or against this body-knowledge.

This is a learned thing for most people, it certainly was for me, but it is absolutely necessary for effective sorcery.

---

2   These are of course not truly separate things, but I am seeking a particular type of information. If someone is good to me, I might feel "happy"…but what does "happy" really feel like as a bodily sensation? Perhaps I feel my body "opening" to the person, and I may feel warm and more relaxed. Conversely, when I am mistreated, I may feel my body contract, tighten up, and feel a heavy feeling in my belly.

CHAPTER SEVEN

RE/CLAIMING: SELF, POWER, AND POSITION

This is my suggested foundational practice for new practitioners. It aims to first cut some ties and attachments[1] that are not helpful, mainly those relating to guilt or shame. Guilt and shame are arguably useful in a social sense, but problematic in a magical one. Secondly, it begins to draw or call back in any stray bits of personal power that have been lost, stolen, or discarded. Lastly, it is a self-blessing and consecration,[2] a claiming of space as a sovereign being. I know many who have made it a lasting part of their daily practices.

A few words about loss of power may be in order here. Although it is not an accurate description, it can be helpful to think for a moment that we each have a finite amount of personal power. This power is what allows us to be who we truly are, to the best of our abilities. We are at our best when this power is all with us, all together, a single unit. When we give our attention to outside forces, unless we draw it back to us, it can after a fashion "stay" where we have placed it, perhaps in a past relationship, or a city in which we used to live. This diminishes what power is available to us for use. It also leaves us almost literally "scattered." Perhaps you have had the experience where work or school interferes with your home life or

---

1   A bit on attachments. To attach is to fasten, fix, to join to, and so attachments refer to those things we are fixed, tied, or bound to, be they objects, people, ideas, or states of being. Most of our attachments are not consciously chosen, or if they were at one time, they may have moved into an unconscious state where we now perceive them as "always has been, always will be" types of things. There is nothing inherently wrong with attachment, but from the sorcerous view, it is in our interest to only stay attached to those things that serve us well! One of the major perks of magical practice is that we can become more able to see where we have attachments that work against our best interest while providing a variety of options the sever, break, or release them.

2   To consecrate means to make or declare something holy. Holy is derived from words meaning sacred, consecrated, venerated, whole, healthy. In magical terms I tend to think of it as "to make special," or to dedicate something or someone to a purpose or deity.

relationships? Even where there is really nothing demanding your attention at that moment? In a sense, we have left some of our power at work or at school, and our inability to focus on what is real and important right now is in part due to this.

Another common way we lose power is through trauma. When we are mistreated or outright abused by someone, they have almost literally claimed some of our power as theirs. This can persist indefinitely unless we reclaim it. To do so will not likely "fix" everything (we might still need therapy or another kind of healing, for example), but by reclaiming our power we can return to our natural, whole state. This allows us to bring all of our innate power to bear on the magic we do. This is necessary for us to do our best work.

Here is the rite. Once or twice a day for a full lunar month is a good schedule in the beginning.

Get a printed photo of yourself. Set it on your altar (any flat surface will do as an altar) along with a bowl of fresh water, a candle, and some incense.

I like to add crushed dried rose petals to the water, but a drop of an essential oil or a spray of a favorite perfume works as well, and plain water is of course fine.

Light the candle, light the incense.

Take a few minutes to calm and center,[3] and relax. Take a few breaths, and then begin.

1. Forgive yourself your failures, out loud. *"I forgive myself my failures, each and every one of them, past, present, and future."* Repeat this section three times every time you do this ritual.

2. After you have done that and felt whatever you felt from it, call back all of your power that has strayed from you in any way. Say *"I call back all of my power.[4] All that was taken from me, all that I gave away, all that I*

---

3   More on this calm and center business in the meditation and trance chapters. For now just breathing deeply for a few minutes is fine.

4   Thanks to Danielle LaPorte for the language of calling back your power.

lost. I call it all back to me. As it was, as it is, and as it shall be." Repeat this section three times every time you do this work.

3. Bless yourself, and give thanks. *"Here and now, ever and always, as an Avatar of the Ineffable,[5] I bless myself. I give thanks to the powers that aid and guard me, I thank them for their help, their protection, and their infinite blessings. As was, as is, as is to come."* Repeat this section three times every time you do this work.

Throughout the work, as inspired, consecrate or bless yourself with the water. This may be a few drops or a full body thing. Give special attention to the whole head (particularly brow, crown, back, nape of the neck), throat, hands, feet, as well as anywhere you find yourself holding pain. Feel free to rewrite what words you say, but don't deviate from the intention, and include some form of the "past, present, future" or "As it was, as it is, and as it shall be."

---

5   Ineffable means that which is beyond expressing in words.

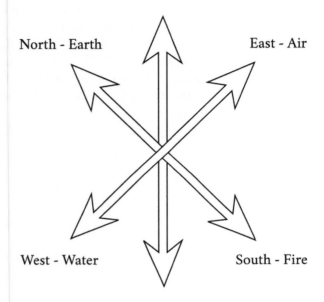

The World Above

North - Earth   East - Air

West - Water   South - Fire

The Underworld

THE SIX WAYS

CHAPTER EIGHT

THE SIX WAYS

The Six Ways[1] is a name for a particular map of reality. It is complex enough to be useful, while simple enough to allow changes to occur organically without disruption to the whole.

We see this general shape (although the name comes from British witchcraft) in many places. We see it in Ceremonial Magic, witchcraft, and in some forms of shamanry.[2] The structure as I use it is as follows.

This is the story: We live in our bodies in Middle World. The Middle World is divided into four directions: North, South, East, and West. The Middle World is viewed as the middle section of a great Tree, whose roots travel deep into the Underworld and whose branches spread wide into the World Above. The worlds Above and Below are actual Otherworlds, in that while they interpenetrate the Middle World, they are fully non-physical (or so it seems from where we dwell).

The Middle World also has its Others, and these are closer to us embodied spirits. Some schools of thought find these "closer in" spirits to be the more dangerous (and conversely often more able to be helpful) to us. I think this is because they partake more of the world we inhabit, and so are able to intervene more intensely in it. We are also more likely to trespass on their turf, so to speak, and thus give offense. I agree with this view, both the helpful and the unhelpful aspects.

Part of the value of this kind of practice and map is that it can be useful to have a "place" for the Powers we interact with to dwell, so that we know where to go if we wish to visit them. It is useful to align the directions to the traditional four elements as used in Western magic: Earth in the

---

1   For chapter and book title I must give thanks to Daniel Bran Griffith, whose book *The Three Nails, the Six Ways, the Stang and the Compass* provided me with the words for this.

2   See Mircea Eliade, *The Sacred and the Profane* for more on this.

North, Air in the East, Fire in the South, and Water in the West.[3] As I often say, it is probably not an accurate description of things, but it is a useful one!

While the map is not the terrain, it is helpful in this case to pretend that it is. What I mean by this is not to get distracted by the physical structures around you and understand that this is an internal, magical compass, not a physical, earthly one.[4] The directions are not cardinal compass points aligned to magnetic North, but to the elemental Powers of the six directions or ways. To begin with, I suggest you leave them where they are even if for you the "actual" water is to the East!

There are many places that will give you lots and lots of magical correspondences for the elements (if you find that you would like them), but for now, I will offer just a few. These are my experiences of these elements and directions, and may not agree with other sources or with what you find to be true for you.

Earth is the solid base, the fertile ground. Earth is slow, heavy, structured, steady, fertile, rooted, grounded. Body and bones. Its nature is nurturing, building, strengthening. Unwavering, stubborn, cold (although fiery hot at its core), filled with mystery. As the Northern element, its time is Midnight and is the home of the Hunt.[5]

Air is fast, flight, whispers, speech, story, mind, thought, communication, breath, truth and deception, words, transitory, informative, data-driven, knowledge, communicative. Mind. Air is warm and moist. Words that cut and words that heal. As the Eastern element its time is Sunrise and it is a place of beginning.

Fire is hot passion, hot blood, transmutation, and transformation. Fire is fast, light, quick, consuming, transforming, passionate, dry, hot. Blood and spirit. Where one thing is changed into another, Spirit and Soul, lust and desire. As the Southern element, its time is Midday.

Water is wet, amniotic, dreaming, oceanic, inexorable, fantastic, wear-

---

3   I should note that while I use a four element model, there are other options.

4   Another way to say this is that in sorcery we work with metaphors "as if" they were true. It may be helpful to decide up front that it is perfectly all right to have multiple maps of reality in play at the same time. This saves us from the mostly futile and nearly always limiting practice of trying to settle on or prove one "correct" model.

5   The Wild Hunt. See Claude Lecouteux, *Phantom Armies of the Night*.

ing, emotional, life-giving, tears, spit, sweat, sexual fluids, carrying, floating, cooling, dreaming, womb and tomb. As the Western element, its time
is Sunset. The Western Gate is also a path to the Land of the Dead.

The World Above, the Heavens, Celestial and Empyrean, the beyond,
the star-home. The Above is the home of the angels, stellar and planetary
powers, it is cold and void, un-human, and removed.

The Below is the Underworld, the lands of the Dead and the Chthonic
Powers, the Stars Below. Warm and often healing, home to faeries, animal
powers, the chthonic daemons, and the wells where the World Tree's roots
are watered. It is an odd place. It is here that I can most easily learn to shift
forms, to be other than human.

THE STARS OF THE SIX WAYS

So with all of that stated, let's look at a directional ritual. This is based on
a ritual magic structure and forms of it also show up in some streams of
witchcraft and Wicca. Feel free to adjust the recipe to suit your own pal-
ate, but if you are new to this kind of thing I suggest doing it as it is written.

Stand[6] and face North. It is best if you say all the words "in quotes"
aloud, even if very quietly. Whisper if needed, but get used to speaking out
loud! Remember that magic is a process of communication.

Take a few breaths to get yourself quiet. Place your hand(s) on your
abdomen just above your groin, and imagine that you are breathing into
the space beneath your hands. Stay with this for a few moments or as long
as makes sense.

Feel, sense, see or otherwise imagine[7] yourself rooted as a tree. You are
a tree. Your roots dig deep into the Earth, and deep into the Below. If you
feel nothing, that is fine. Just tell yourself *"I am rooted like the Tree, deep
into the Earth. My roots reach deep into the realms Below. The Earth-light, the*

---

6   If you cannot stand or if doing so is very difficult, you can of course sit. Much of my
     work is done seated, it is no problem whatsoever.

7   In all cases where I suggest visualizing, sensing, imagining – this can happen through
     any sense. If you are unable to sense any level of this part of work at first, don't
     worry. Some folks have an innate knack for it, for others it takes more time. I am fairly
     non-gifted in this way.

Earth-fire nourishes me, and feeds me with the powers from the Underworld."
Stay with this for a few moments, or as long as it makes sense to remain.

Now bring your hands to the top of your skull. Feel the pull of the
Above, drawing you taller, and feel yourself standing straighter. Know
that you as the Tree are extended high up into the realms Above, and that
your limbs spread wide, and that your leaves collect the Starlight that falls
upon them. If you feel or see nothing, that is fine. Just tell yourself "*I am
like a great tree, my limbs reach for the Heavens, my branches spread wide,
reaching in all directions and always towards the Stars Above. The Stellar
Light, the Star-fire rains down upon me and nourishes me with the powers
from the Above.*" Stay with this for a few moments, or as long as it makes
sense to remain.

Now begin to address the directions. You may turn and face them if you
are standing, or do this turning and facing part internally in your imagination if you are sitting or lying down.

Face North, and speak: "*Powers of the North, I call out to you. Come into
this place. Gift me with the Powers of Earth.*" Raise your hands, palms out,
to the Northern, Earthy Powers.

Face East, and speak: "*Powers of the East, I call out to you. Come into this
place. Gift me with the Powers of Air.*" Raise your hands, palms out, to the
Eastern, Airy Powers.

Face South, and speak: "*Powers of the South, I call out to you. Come into
this place. Gift me with the Powers of Fire.*" Raise your hands, palms out, to
the Southern, Fiery Powers.

Face West, and speak: "*Powers of the West, I call out to you. Come into this
place. Gift me with the Powers of Water.*" Raise your hands, palms out, to the
Western, Watery Powers.

Turn back to the North to finish:

Address the Above: "*Powers of the World Above, come into this place. Gift
me with the Stellar Powers.*" Raise your palms to the sky, to the Powers of
the Above.

Address the Below: "*Powers of the Underworld, come into this place. Gift
me with the Chthonic Powers.*" Face your palms towards the ground, to the
Powers of the Below.

If there is something you need or other magical work you will do here, do it or ask for it now. It is also totally fine to simply speak of what is going on and what you would like help with. I'm not fancy about this. Here is an example:

I am a bit worried about my business right now, and could use some help and guidance keeping it and myself on the right track and focused on the things that will best help me to move forward.

This is also a good space to ask questions via divination. Remember, whenever you ask for help or pose a question, give time for an answer to show itself. It may not show right away, but it just might, and you are squandering an opportunity if you don't take the time to see!

To close the working space, stand in the center and say:

By the Stars in the North
By the Stars in the South
By the Stars in the East
By the Stars in the West
By the Stars Above
By the Stars Below
I thank you for your aid and guidance, may there be peace between us for all of our days.

The reader may notice a few things in the "Stars" ritual. There are no gods, spirits, or angelic forms addressed by name. This is quite by design, as I personally believe that we are attended to by many Powers on an individual level. I am not about to suggest you need to or should work with my people! I also don't personally find it important to "name" most of the beings I work with: as one of them told me recently when I asked about a name, "I am not a dog, I won't come when you call, you know where to find me."

That said, you are of course welcome to insert the names of the Powers you work with in the places they fit. This could be adding the Archangels, the "Guardians of the Watchtowers" from some streams of witchcraft, what have you. It is not generally important but may be specifically important to you.

What is generally important is to build a practice of asking the Powers of the Elements and the Above and Below to come into the place you inhabit when you do the work. This both forges connections with the various powers and is a request for their presence in your life.

Look at it like this: If I operate within the framework of my purely material existence then to the East is the highway, the West is the Air Force Base, to the North is the High School and to the South is the wrong side of the tracks. The power lines are above and the pavement below. It is neither inspiring nor helpful to view things this way from a magical perspective. That it may be literally true (in one world!) has no bearing on its usefulness from a magical perspective.

The first and most important enchantment is the enchantment of the world, which by its very nature is also the enchantment of us, its perceiver. A large amount of the work of magic and sorcery as I have come to know it has to do with this concept.[8]

By starting with the decision that there is at the very least the possibility of magic, of elemental powers, and of other realms above and below, I begin to load the world I inhabit with possibilities.

If there is a place of power called North, that I can look towards, that I know a little about, its relation to Earth, its nature as a cold, steady, calming, grounding place, then I have the possibility of traveling to that place. I have the possibility of drawing things to me from that place. I have the possibility of making contact with those who inhabit that place. I have the possibility of mutual aid with those beings. Multiply this by the Six Ways, and I have many options for learning, aid, exploration, ways of thinking, and ways of being.

---

8 This is also why magical aesthetics are of high importance. These will vary greatly depending on the practitioner, but time and energy spent to get it "right" visually or sensually, whatever "right" is for you, will pay out very quickly.

CHAPTER NINE

ENTERING INTO SILENCE

There are three main pieces of "work" or skills that are foundational to the practice of magic as I practice it. Work is what you do, your actual actions. Magic is based on work. Thought, research, and study are not magic until they turn into action, until you actually do the work. None of these three skills are particularly sexy, at least not at the beginning. They are breath work (or pranayama), meditation, and trance.

Like it or not, healthy or not, free of pain or not, we are living in and therefore working our magic through our bodies. As long as we are living, our body sustains us to the best of its ability and is the root filter for our experience. Our body may be unwell, filled with pain or anxiety, or unable to sustain its own life without outside intervention, and this is still true.

To get a handle on our psychic selves (mind, soul, spirit) we have to do so through the medium of our body. This entails learning to relax, first by evening out our breathing. This breath work is what allows meditation and trance to occur. It allows for deep relaxation, and release of tension patterns first in the body, and then in the mind. It allows us to become aware of the energy systems of the body/mind/spirit/soul complex and to influence it to our benefit, instead of letting it operate in unhelpful or dysfunctional patterns.

To start, find a way to sit comfortably with your spine fairly straight, meaning that you aren't hunched forward or slouched back, but pretty well upright. Sitting in a chair is fine. Once you are seated, place your hands on either your knees or thighs (palms can be up or down), folded in your lap or another place where they can rest comfortably. I use a pretty standard half-lotus meditation posture, but it took some time for that to become truly comfortable. I find sitting on a folded up towel or blanket about three inches thick really helps me to find a comfortable posture when sitting on the floor.

If you are able to sit fairly comfortably and with a sense of stability, all is well.

Now breathe through your nose, in and out. To start with, if it is painful just to sit, only do this for a few minutes at a time. Five minutes at a time is enough to begin with. When I first began doing this work, the process was a bit painful, as I didn't have the muscular strength and flexibility to sit truly upright for any length of time. In time and with practice your body will come to find its right alignment and gain the strength and flexibility it needs.

Keep breathing through your nose, in and out. Now decide to even out your inhalations and exhalations. Notice which one is longer, in or out, and match the shorter breath to the longer. Counting can help with this. So perhaps you notice that you inhale for a four count and exhale for a three count. Gently extend your exhale to a four count. No need to push, there is no actual problem here. It's all about attention, and time. Once you have your breaths equalized, extend them by a count. So now you are breathing in a five-five count, in this example.

Spend some time there. Notice what you feel. Do your ribs expand a bit more? Are there any spots of resistance? What part of your lungs does it feel like you are breathing into? The top, middle, or bottom?

See if by shifting your attention you can move your breath more deeply into the parts of your lungs you are not using as much of. For me, this is always first about breathing more deeply into my lower lungs, which makes my belly expand. I move my attention to allowing my belly to relax and expand out with each breath. Once my belly is moving smoothly in and out as I breathe, I move my attention to filling the rest of my lungs fully, but without strain, always first filling into the bottom, then the middle, and then the top.

Once you are breathing in a smooth, even pattern, using the full volume of your lungs (whatever that is for you right now, it will change with practice), see if you can gently add a pause on each "end" of the breathing cycle. Make it brief, and don't try to choke off your breath. Instead, just let a space form. Inhale, two, three, four, five, pause, exhale, two, three, four, five, pause. Cycle this for a while, and see if you can smooth out the whole pattern.

This pattern, of lengthening the in and out breath without forcing it, and then adding pauses and lengthening them, is the foundational practice of the breath. This can be continued to whatever degree seems helpful. At times I work just on really filling the lungs, relaxing the muscles in my torso until my ribs expand freely. At other times I work on extending the length of the breaths, the pauses, or the cycle overall. All of these practices will have their own effects on both the body and the mind.

If you are just starting, sit and consciously breathe for at least five minutes twice a day to begin, and in time extend that. I try to get in twenty minutes a day in whatever way it works out. I sometimes use a string of beads or mala to count breaths, but setting a timer works as well.

In time, there are many other patterns or ways of breathing that can be helpful. But this is the basis, and all that is really needed for the work that I do.

If you are doing the breath work, you are already meditating. Meditation has a huge amount of variations, intentions, and rules depending on where you learn it and what your focus is. I'm not much into the rules about it, as I think it is an organic process that we have simply lost the knack of in the modern age.

At its root, to meditate is to "sit down and shut up." The sitting down is straightforward, the "shutting up" is less so!

Back to the breath. If you are able to mainly focus on your breath (in fits and starts if you are at all like me!), perhaps the sounds of it, or the feel of it in your nostrils, or the feel of it in entering and leaving your body, your mind will quiet a bit. For some, they will easily slide into a quieter space. For most people, the talking, looping (also called "discursive," meaning rambling or digressing) part of the mind will decide to have a bit of a fit, as it is unused to being un-entertained. So it will do its thing and start to tell a litany of stories. These stories are of no importance in the moment, as you are doing something else. But they will roll on and on, vying for attention. The best way to slow these loops down is not to try to stop them, but to "notice them." I do this using a method I picked up from *vipassana* or insight meditation. In this kind of meditation, we only really have a few categories of thought/experience. You are either thinking about and replaying the past, which we call "remembering," thinking about the future, which we call "fantasizing," or feeling something (either physically or emotionally, like an itch or sadness) which is "feeling." You may find that you feel the need for more labels, but keep them simple and direct. Feeling, tasting, smelling, touching, projecting, and the like. Otherwise, you are sitting with the rising and falling of the breath, you are experiencing the moment, which we don't label anything.

For this basic meditation, as the mind tells you its stories, instead of engaging in conversation about them, just note them and sort of file them away. So when an old argument you had or a great experience you had rises up in your thoughts, instead of diving into it or having an opinion about it, simply internally say "remembering" and return to your breathing. There is no need to force anything away or "shut down your thinking," just notice the thoughts arising, and then return your focus to your breath.

Perhaps your nose itches. You can just notice this "nose itching." Inhale, exhale. Try not to get too detailed, just simply notice what is going on, then return to what you are actually doing, which is sitting quietly and breathing. Some sources will tell you to ignore all phenomena like itches, but if it is persistent, I make a conscious decision to scratch it, actually scratch it, and then return focus to the breath afterwards.

At first, this can seem like a total train wreck, like the mind is a pit of twisting serpentine thoughts, all past or future tense, nothing of the now. This is the shape of the discursive mind. Its function is to describe what it experiences, be these real events, memories, or outright fantasies. This is totally normal, and for most people, it never really goes completely away. What mostly happens is that we learn to turn down the volume. I experience this as very much like turning down the sound on a stereo while it is playing. The sound just fades lower and lower into the background, and eventually is so quiet it is no longer perceptible.

When I first began the process of this kind of meditation, where I noticed my thoughts as memories or fantasies, it took a few months of noticing my thoughts (and filing them using the labels mentioned earlier) before I got any real "headspace" from it. Those months were in no way wasted time! What I found was that although I was noticing the (fucking endless stream of) thoughts and memories, they pretty rapidly became less engaging. I began to see that they were not really happening at all in any location except my mind. I began to see that they were all projections of past or future, or simple sensations (hunger, cold). They weren't really important to focus on in any way. They were just something my mind was experiencing and telling itself about.

For example, let's say that I am meditating and the memory of an old horrible boss will intrude. And I get angry! So now I am thinking of this old boss and I am angry. I notice what is happening, which is I am *remembering* something past and *feeling* things because of this memory. I note "remembering" and let it fade, and if need be, if I am really riled up from it, I will notice "feeling anger" and let that fade as well. This will seem impossible, stupid, and dishonest to some at first. Ride this out, and in time you will see that these things are true. That old boss is not present now. He is not being an evil prick to you right now. These are memories, which are like echoes of events. The event is long past. So will you be angry at this echo? Will this echo be equal in importance to what you feel right now? What if instead, we notice the remembering, notice the anger and get back to now? This is a small piece of freedom, and one worth working for.

As things progressed for me, and things did progress pretty quickly (quickly meaning months, not days or weeks), I'd find these little gaps, where I was just breathing, and there was nothing to notice, no remembering or fantasizing. I was just breathing, and sort of watching myself breathe. These gaps were very calm and very quiet. Some days they were longer, some days shorter. This is still true today.

So make a decision (and that is all that it is) to sit, and to breathe, and to notice your thoughts. This decision will lead to a place, or many places, or states, if you do the work and put in the time. If all you get from it is a few momentary gaps of quiet most days, you will be well on your way to a much greater control of your mind, and much greater levels of ease and relaxation.

The next useful type of meditation is a concentration meditation. I tend to do this with a small item to gaze upon. A candle or stone, or a coyote or bobcat skull. I prefer to do it in dim light, or with a single candle if it is dark, but I also do this while sitting in the sun at times.

Sit in your upright posture, and set your focus item (we will use the candle for example) where your gaze rests on it comfortably. Now begin to breathe. Slow and deepen the breath. Tell yourself *"I breathe in, and relax. I breathe out, becoming calm."* Let your gaze settle on the candle. Just gaze at it, and breathe. It can help (and this is true in the earlier meditation form as well) to note your breath as "rising" or "falling." Just sit, and gaze at the candle. If your vision "splits" and doubles the image, bring the focus back to the candle. This is all there is to it. In time, you may drift, lose sight of the candle completely, or have a sudden rush of thoughts. Just note the breath, rising and falling, and return to the candle.

There are of course a vast number of ways to meditate. These methods are simple and easy to learn, and will do what we need them to do for the work outlined in this book.

CHAPTER TEN

ENTERING INTO TRANCE

To become aware of the Otherworld that we share with the less generally obvious powers, we must learn to shift our normal methods of perception a bit. The available and traditional methods range from drugs and sensory deprivation to exhaustion, pain, sex, breath control, meditation, fasting, music, trance and multiples of these things in combination. The easiest way I know of is through simple relaxation and light trance induction.

There is a common perception that trance states are "all or nothing." That I am either in a heavy, deep trance, with no perception of my body or normal reality, or I am not in a trance state at all. The reality is far more varied, the edges far more blurred. The trance state as suggested here can be very heavy, totally immersive, or quite light and subtle. The only real requirement is to become very still and deeply relaxed, without actually falling asleep.

For myself, I can define three levels of trance that are all normal and all useable.

The first I think of as "light trance," in that I am quite relaxed, not at all twitchy, and sort of softly "drifting." I've still got full awareness of my body, I can feel any breeze on my skin, and I don't have a clear sense of anything truly non-ordinary. This is a great space to meditate in! As I am really still and my mind is really quiet, it's actually easier than my usual sitting meditation. In this first state I tend to do a lot of "head cleaning," just softly noticing and clearing attachments or releasing worries.

The second state I think of as a "full trance." I am deeply relaxed, I have less of a sense of my own body, and the physical world is rather muffled or muted. I feel like I am floating in space, or on the surface of a warm, dark ocean. Here I am much more able to contact spirits and Others, and may get "almost audio" information.[1] In this state I do a lot of energy work and healing type work. This is a great place to "plant" ideas that I would like to

---

1 By "almost audio" I mean that I am receiving information via language, but I am not

internalize, and to seek out what I think of as "buried programs." Buried programs are my term for old psychic and emotional drivers, things that are always running on an unconscious level. Most of them are not helpful, and so finding them is a good first step to clearing them out to improve quality of mind and life.

The third state is what I think of as "deep trance." Here I am way more than relaxed, and it takes a conscious effort to "rise up" into my body to move my limbs. The sensation is of being comfortably but exceedingly heavy (which is totally comfortable), and fully in the Otherworld. I am on and off aware of my body; it really depends on the session. Here I can walk, run, fly, pick up objects, get into a river, turn into an animal, make a mud-toy, or whatever is happening during that visit. In deep trance I can inter-act in a "mostly as normal" fashion with spirits, allies, and Others.[2] I can visit the elemental realms, the Underworld, or the World Above. While this is the most immersive and intense level of the trance experience, it is not always the goal. All three states are totally useful and beneficial.

I tend to drift in and out of these different depths of trance, even within a single session.[3] If it seems like you "can't get deep enough," simply work with where you are and assume that the process is working. Stress is not your ally here, so be very easy on yourself and have gentle expectations!

This is a method of trance induction I was taught that works very well. I have used variations of it for almost thirty years.

TRANCE INDUCTION

Sit comfortably with your back fairly straight. You can also do this lying down, but falling asleep may be an issue. I personally do it lying down for "traveling work" and sitting up for more outright magical working. I also tend to have half an hour to an hour of wakefulness a few nights a week around 3 A.M., and I prefer to spend that time in trance rather than trying to get back to sleep right away.

---

really hearing it, it is simply forming in my mind as if it is spoken.

2   Anyone who has played here will I think agree that "mostly as normal" is an absurd statement, but it's the best description I can come up with!

3   This is somewhat dependent on how involved the cat decides to be in the process.

To begin, start talking to yourself internally as follows, imagining that what you are saying is wholly true, even if you do not "feel it" at first. Try to pace this so that the first part of the sentence happens on the inhalation and the part after the comma on the exhalation.

I breathe deeply, and my breathing deepens with each breath. I breathe deeply, and feel my heart rate slow. I breathe deeply, and I feel my entire body relax completely.

My head is warm and heavy, my head is sinking into the ground.
My face is warm and heavy, my face is sinking into the ground.
My jaw is warm and heavy, my jaw is sinking into the ground.
My neck and shoulders are warm and heavy, my neck and shoulders are sinking into the ground.
My chest and back are warm and heavy, my chest and back are sinking into the ground.
My belly is warm and heavy, my belly is sinking into the ground.
My hips are warm and heavy, my hips are sinking into the ground.
My arms and legs are warm and heavy, my arms and legs are sinking into the ground.
My hands and feet are warm and heavy, my hands and feet are sinking into the ground.

Some people will at this point be deep in trance, a state of quiet, stillness, and calm. If you are still a bit agitated and wiggly, continue as follows:

My head is dissolving into darkness.
My face is dissolving into darkness.
My jaw is dissolving into darkness.
My neck and shoulders are dissolving into darkness.
My chest and back are dissolving into darkness.
My belly is dissolving into darkness.
My hips are dissolving into darkness.
My arms and legs are dissolving into darkness.
My hands and feet dissolving into darkness.

The third stage (if needed, and these stages all tend to get shorter and collapse together if practice is regular, but may need to be worked in series when you are starting out or agitated) is this:

My head is floating in silence.
My face is floating in silence.
My jaw is floating in silence.
My neck and shoulders are floating in silence.
My chest and back are floating in silence.
My belly is floating in silence.
My hips are floating in silence.
My arms and legs are floating in silence.
My hands and feet are floating in silence.

That should do it for most people. Some people may find that they need to do this daily for a while before they can feel comfortable enough to release their tension and anxiety. This is normal, and nothing to worry about. It can also help to talk to any areas of the body that are still too "active." Sometimes I will tell my feet (or any other body part) that they are "happy, well, and comfortably settled into place" if I need to.[4]

There is another approach that will work more easily for some people. This style I learned from Jan Fries.[5] This is a very easy approach and well worth a try!

Here is a basic induction. Speak internally as before, one short section on each inhalation and exhalation:

I breathe deeply – and relax completely – as I breathe – I notice that –
my heart rate slows – and my jaw relaxes – and I am very still – and

---

4   If you really have a hard time getting into this state try these things. Try entering the trance lying flat on your back, and it can help to elevate the legs slightly with a pillow under your knees. You may also try laying a heavy blanket over your body. Sometimes placing a pillow over the chest and belly can give a better sense of being "grounded" and held and really help. I find it helps to have the tips of my thumbs and middle fingers touching (on each hand, think of the typical images of a meditating yogini or monk). As I have a lot of animals around and am quite sensitive to sound, I usually wear earplugs.

5   Jan Fries, *Visual Magick: A Manual of Freestyle Shamanism.*

each breath – takes me deeper – into a quiet – and very still – relaxed
state – I breathe in – and notice – that my hands – and my arms –
that my feet – and my legs – are very warm – and very heavy – and
are sinking into – the warm earth – which enfolds me – and comforts
me – and my belly – and my chest – my head and my neck – my back
and my shoulders – are all very warm – and are all sinking – into the
soft – warm earth – as I breathe in – I sink deeper – and deeper – into
the earth – until I am – completely relaxed – floating – in the warm
darkness – in the softness of space – etc., etc. Continue on until you are
at the level of trance you wish to be in.

If you are relaxed and still, continue onto the next section. If not, cycle
through the above again until you are. Although this is a simple process, it
is not always easy. These things take time and practice to learn.

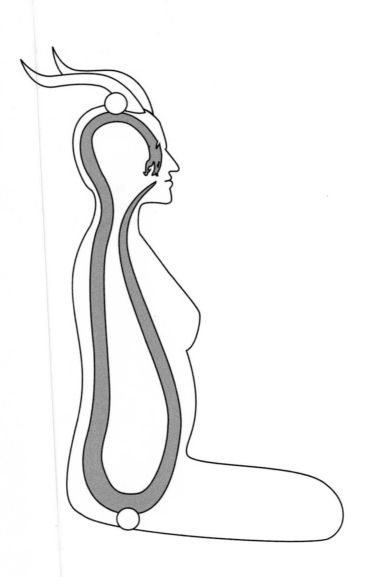

THE MICROCOSMIC ORBIT

CHAPTER ELEVEN

ENTERING INTO POWER

ORBITAL

This practice is easiest to perform sitting upright.

So you should now be somewhat zoned out, and very quiet inside. I want you to notice two points on your body (often called chakras), one at your perineum, hereafter called the "root," and one at the very top of your skull, hereafter called the "crown."[1]

Become aware (this is something that is already happening, but you may need practice to become fully aware of it) that there is a pattern of energy orbiting inside your body. It is like a long loop that starts at the root chakra and rises to the crown chakra, rising inside of you close to the back side of the body when you inhale, and as you exhale it falls from the crown back down to the root, traveling inside your body close to your front side. Just breathe in and maintain awareness of that looping cycle, inhale and exhale, rising root to crown, and falling from the crown back to root, endless.

In the image of the orbit, you will notice a gap in the orbit in the mouth. To complete the orbit, you touch the tip of the tongue to the roof of the mouth behind the front teeth. The exact point is not critical, but making that connection is. An interesting side note is that when we are talking a lot, this completion of the orbit can't really be maintained.

If that is fairly clear – and some will see this in full color and 3D, some will see it as hazy, and some won't see it at all and will feel it or perceive it in some other way – move onto the next step. How exactly this perception

---

1   This is a borrowing from Taoist alchemy, and is called the microcosmic orbit. It is something I first learned in the 1980's and returned to a few years ago under the influence of Jason Miller.

starts is not really important. What I am after is a clear sense of the orbit moving in the body, the specific sense that perceives it is not that important. In time and with practice perception of the orbit will strengthen and clarify. This may take days or months of repetition, which is fine. This is a learning process, and like building muscle it takes time. Awareness will come at different rates for everyone, but it will come.

If you have awareness of the orbit spinning inside of you, you can next become aware of two more things.

First, notice that there is another orbit, this one outside of you and below you. It cycles through the Earth below, carrying a deep current of earth-fire. It meets the orbit inside of you at the root point. You realize that this earth-fire orbit actually feeds your inner orbit, providing solid, grounded power to you.

Sit with that for a bit, and once you have a good sense of it, continue.

While maintaining your awareness of the earth-fire orbit and your inner orbit, you notice another orbit outside of you.

This orbit is immense, dwarfing even the earth-fire orbit. It cycles through the universe at large, and you notice that it intersects with your inner orbit at the crown point. It feeds your inner orbit with stellar energy, star-fire. This is a clear, focused energy.

You come to realize that these two upper and lower orbits provide a fuel source to you through the root and crown points, a readily available power source as well as a source of continuous connection to the Field at large.

Here are some things that I have found that can be done with the orbits:

Turn your palms to face each other, and become aware that you have energy centers in the middle of each palm.

Notice that you can feel an orbit that passes through your arms and into the palms, making a circuit.

Bring your hands close together, as if they are holding a small ball. Feel the energy from the orbit filling that ball.

Once you have a strong sense of this ball, open your eyes just slightly, just enough to see your hands but not clearly. Watch the space between your hands. Some people will see light, some a sort of haze, some a visual distortion, like a shimmer.

Know that you can use this energy that is moving through your hands. You can place your hands onto your body and use the energy to provide healing, or place it into an object to create a bond with it and empower it.

You can speak into your hands to fill the power there with an intention, and then turn your palms out to project that intention into the Field.

You can fill your hands with power and then "feed" it to a spirit you are working with as an offering or form of information transmission.

There are many ways to work with this energy, but these should be enough to get you started.

FIRE SNAKES

This practice is easiest to perform sitting upright or standing.

This is a more visceral variation of the Orbital work. I use it for most active magical work, and the Orbital for more meditative work.

Do the Trance Induction (or whatever version or form of it that you have developed to achieve the same state).

Once you are settled, sense that you are rooted like a tree. That you are a tree. That you are the World Tree. You are the crossroads between the Stars. You are the intersection between what was, what is, and what is to come. You are the nexus of the crisis, the origin of storms.[2] Now send your consciousness downward in a call to the powers of the Below. You feel a response from deep in the hot center of the Earth. A great serpentine force, ruddy red with magma-light, filled with earth-fire comes rising from below and moves into you. This is a massive, potent, forceful energy that fills you up, feet, legs, groin, belly, rising into your chest and from there up into your arms, shoulder, neck and head. This is strong, energizing power, healing to the physical structures of your body.

As the earth-fire serpent reaches the crown of your head, it calls out to its Stellar counterpart. The Star-fire Serpent descends through the top of

---

2   *Astronomy*, Blue Öyster Cult. Yes, I use song lyrics in my ritual work all the time. While some get their kicks from talking like they are in *The Lord of the Rings* and others will happily crib bits and pieces from ancient Egypt or Greece, I will be busy dropping parts of BOC and Motorhead songs in my work (and my chapter titles).

your head, flooding your body with blue-white stellar light. This Star-fire fills you from top to bottom, from crown to root, through arms, hands, shoulders and chest then down through belly, groin, legs and feet. The star-fire purifies and heals all the non-physical structures of your being that it comes in contact with. The twin snakes spiral together throughout the body, burning off impurities, healing illnesses, clearing you of demonic intrusions and any stray tendrils of unhelpful power that have attached to you in your day to day life.

Draw (imagine) the twin serpents into a fiery ball at belly level. Know that you will hold onto exactly the amount of their power as your current capacity will allow, thank them, and release them. Sense them leaving your body, sense the ball of energy that still rests inside you, and either close[3] or move on to the next piece of work.

---

3 Closing is any kind of formal "ending" to a piece of work. I usually release the last of the energy, and quietly say "thank you" or "blessings to you" and then return to the wake-world.

CHAPTER TWELVE

TRANCE AND TRAVELING

The trance state is itself a healing state, allowing for deep levels of relaxation. It also allows for what is called guided (or unguided!) visualization, active imagination, journeying or traveling. These terms are largely interchangeable. What they refer to is a shift of focus and perception from the outer, clearly physical and mundane world, the ordinary reality, to an inner world or Otherworld, the non-ordinary reality.[1] These are tools that help us to enter the Otherworld, the in-between and threshold states of reality, and interface with both our own deep minds and the Others.

Here are some entries to places I travel to while in trance that are good starting points for further exploration.

THE TREE

(If you are not coming from the Fire Snakes practice, and have not already done so, perform the Induction.)

Once you are settled, sense that you are rooted like a tree. That you are a tree. That you are the World Tree.

You grow at a crossroads, two well-traveled paths in the center of an ancient forest. Yet you are the First Tree. You are massive in comparison to the trees around you, and far older. You are aware of your roots, sunk deep into the very ground of being, extending deep into the Underworld. Your roots twist serpentine through vast caverns, feeding on underground pools, lakes and rivers filled with strange creatures who rest and hunt among them. You are fed information, insight, visions via these roots, via

---

1 These are peculiar concepts and the language can be tricky. There is to me a part of this work that happens "in my consciousness," but there is a large-scale interpenetration that is "not me" as well. It is clear to me that while I set the stage, there are Other players involved! While I am sure some will argue "it's all fantasy," this is a largely irrelevant and unhelpful viewpoint from a magical perspective.

these lakes and pools and rivers. You can hear the echoes of the voices of the past in the vast caverns your roots have wrought.

(If you are seeking knowledge from the Below, you can reach out via your roots to find it here.)

Now shift your focus from your roots and the worlds below to your trunk as it rises, huge beyond measure, rising up up up through Middle World and into the world Above. Your branches spread and shade the world below. Whole ecosystems and microclimates flourish and shift as you move your awareness upwards. As your point of view reaches your canopy, it is cold and dark, and the Stars of Infinite Space shine down upon you. Your leaves are silvered by star-fire, and they absorb both stellar light and pure information from the heavens and feed it into you.

(If you are seeking knowledge from the Above, you can send a call out from here and the stars will shine it down on you.)

Now you become aware of your entire self, roots and trunk and branches and leaves. Rest in this for as long as seems good to you.

When you are finished, for a moment you have a clear impression of yourself, the Fire Snakes inside of you, and you-as-Tree.

Close as desired.

THE WATCHTOWER

This is a visionary space where I go to work magic in the Otherworld, where I won't be distracted by the environment too much.

After the Induction, imagine that you are standing before a door inset in the curving stone wall of a tower. "See" the door as best you can, either as a full on visual or by describing it to yourself. Notice if it is squared off or rounded at the top. Notice if the door handle is on the left or right side. Notice if it will swing inward or outward when you open it. Notice the shape of the handle.

Make the decision to open the door, and grasp the handle. Notice the cool metal of the handle as you open the door.

With the door open wide, you see that it opens up into an entry hall. Notice the floor, the walls. Again, if you do not "see" anything, internally describe what you *might* see if you did. This is fine and normal, and will have no real effect on the process.

Make the decision to enter the tower, and step forward. How many steps forward until you are fully inside?

Notice that there are doorways in the hall that leads to stairs, one on the right and one on the left. One set of stairs leads up to a room higher in the tower, and one leads down to a room under the earth. Notice which set of stairs leads up and which leads down, right or left. Which do you choose? When you have decided to ascend or descend, move to that set of stairs.

Whichever set of stairs you chose, you will find that there are nine steps, up or down, at the end of which is another door. Beyond each door is a working room, mostly plain and empty for now.[2]

The upper room has a table in it with a candle on it, a stick of incense in a holder, and a box of wooden matches. Greet the room, and make offering to it by lighting the candle with the matches, and then lighting the incense from the candle.

The lower room has a stone tomb in it, and a stone table which is set at waist height. On the table is an unlit candle, a stick of incense in a holder, and a box of wooden matches. Greet the room, and make offering to it by lighting the candle with the matches, and then lighting the incense from the candle.

Re-visit these rooms as you desire, and in time you can change them to suit your nature. Perhaps there are windows in the upper room from which you can see the worlds beyond the watchtower. Perhaps there are tunnels branching out from the lower chamber, leading into other realms.

In time you may choose to furnish these rooms, or perhaps you will leave them bare. I have an altar space in each, and am always interested to

---

2   One of my first readers, Dre Achilleus, wrote in response to this section something that is so helpful I asked her permission to include her words. She says: "Ok. You want to hear an example of how literal my brain can be during these exercises? You describe the two doors and sets of stairs. One going to a room higher up, and the other leading to a room under the earth. And then you say that whichever you choose, there are 9 steps. And the first thing that happens is that my brain says, 'There's no way 9 steps could get you down far enough to have a room under the earth. The ceiling would be way too low. That's architecturally impossible.' OMG. Please laugh. This is why when I do shamanic journeying, I have to first consciously turn off my 'analyzer'. I picture myself taking it out of my brain, turning it off, saying thank you, giving it a kiss, and then tucking it into my back pocket. And I do this over and over and over until it calms the hell down and lets me get on with things." Dre makes a fabulous point: remember, you too can choose to turn off your "analyzer" and put it away for a while!

see what item or figure or deity inhabits the central position on the altar when I enter.

MOVING THE SELF

(If not coming to this practice from the Fire Snakes, do the Induction first) Post Induction, which is really establishing a base of deep relaxation where we have bypassed the looping of the discursive mind, there are many ways to go.

I am not giving a program here, as I believe there is more to be learned by exploration. Instead, I will give suggestions for a number of ways to play in this state. I am including them as a numbered list for ease, as they both build on each other and are also discrete approaches you can try.[3]

1   Notice that your consciousness is "seated" somewhere in your body. Try moving it to another point. For me this is usually from the head downward to a lower point.

2   Once you have moved the consciousness point, spend some time noticing what is different from this position. Are you quieter inside? Do you feel more stable? Less stable? Do you feel more emotional? Less emotional? How have your perceptions changed?

3   Notice that you (if you?) have something like a second self, a less physical body that rests inside of or like an overlay on your body. What is that like? Can you feel how they are connected? Can you move your point of consciousness into that body? Is it already present in that body?

4   Can you gently raise that second self up a bit, or move it forward if you

3   I say "you can try" very intentionally. This moving of the apparent location of the consciousness (points 1–6) is a very peculiar set of entries! Please only proceed from a very solid base in trance work, be doing your regular protection work, and decide for yourself if this work is appropriate for you. I've never had any issues with this kind of thing, but I have known a few folks who have. I can't give a prescription here, but if you find the process disturbing or scary I'd set this part aside for the moment, and return to it after a few months of further work and see how it feels at that time.

are sitting or standing? Maybe an inch at a time, an inch per breath? Maybe move it two to four inches, just enough that you can sense the differences between it and your physical body. How are they connected? How do you perceive the second self? Is it dark, light, a mix? How "solid" does it seem?

5   Can you "flip" your perception so that your second self is looking down on your body (assuming you are lying down)? If so, try to "scan" or otherwise sense how your body is doing. Maybe your second self can reach "down" to your body and provide healing?

6   See if from this perspective in the second self you can find energy leaks in your body, places where you can sense your energy or power drifting away, sort of like air leaving a pinhole in an air mattress. Can you close those leaks? I just run my "hands" over my body and sort of gently touch any weak spots which heals them.

7   Crossroads work.[4] When you are deep in trance, begin to notice what exists in the four directions. For me there is a big mountain rising in the North, plains to the East, desert to the South, and a very wet and misty land to the West eventually leading to the sea.

8   In each of these directions, from the center of the crossroads runs a road or path. You can walk into these elemental and perhaps mythic "lands" to explore, learn, and make allies.

9   Allies are present in all of these zones that I have ever visited. When I first enter a zone or realm, I set the intention of meeting the ally. I spend some time communing with the ally. Sometimes they speak, sometimes they show me things, sometimes they act as guides to other places or beings. Know that they are there, and include them in your intentions[5].

---

4   This form of the crossroads work is highly influenced by Brianna Saussy's methods in her excellent Miracle Tree Sessions.

5   I can hear the screams of some practitioners that this is not precisely controlled and safe. Such is life!

10 The work that happens in these other planes can have effects on this one. These effects can be mild or intense. Make only the agreements that make sense to make. You do not have to deal with everyone you meet in these realms any more than you have to deal with everyone you meet in ordinary reality.

11 Not everyone is very visually oriented in these places, myself included. I do see things, but slowly, and the formation of a visual experience can take a lot of time. If this is the case for you as well, it helps to go very easy on yourself. There is no need to stress about this. Vision is only one sense. I've yet to hear anyone complain about not being able to smell clearly in the Otherworld! We are a largely vision-centered culture, but all of the senses can be used for perception. Sometimes what helps is to let yourself sort of describe what you are experiencing, very gently, and not embellishing too much.[6]

12 An example might help. Let's imagine we are in trance, and at the Crossroads. Pick a starting direction, and describe what you would see. It's perfectly OK to keep it very simple and stark. Let say we have picked North. If you don't quickly slip into a visual space, begin to tell yourself what you would be seeing. Here is what the North might be for me: *"I am on the path leading North, the Earth realm. Before me is a great mountain, peak jutting into the sky above me. The road quickly disappears into a dense forest in front of me. I begin to move forward along the road, and enter into the forest. The trees are close by, and very old. I can sense life around me, small creatures all around. I can sense the spirits of the forest, attentive to my entry. I feel the presence of an ally who can help me in this realm. As I move forward, I move closer to the ally."* In time (and that is a very wide open statement) you will develop your senses to explore with more surety. You may not ever "see" these things as others do, but you will come to know them and be able to navigate within them.

---

6 If you find over time that you remain "not sensitive" or "not imaginative" or "not visual" enough to suit yourself in these practices, I suggest working with the exercises in Jan Fries' *Visual Magick* and/or *How To See Fairies* by Ramsey Dukes.

13   Ask allies you meet to guide you. Often an ally can travel in ways other spirits cannot, and can lead you to those that are more home-bound to a locale.

14   It helps to come up with a "moving" language to tell yourself what you are doing as regards to locomotion in the Otherworlds. I currently use "walk forward" a lot, which I learned from Bri Saussy, and as I nearly always start at the Crossroads or Tree, and "return to the Crossroads" or "return to the Tree" when I would like to exit more quickly.

15   Details can help or hinder. While it is easy to get lost in the leaves of a tree (which is not in itself a bad thing), sometimes noting how water droplets sit on a leaf, or how grasses move in a breeze are just the ticket to fully embrace where you are.

16   It is good idea to expect some of what happens in your traveling to slip into your dream states.

17   You can do ritual work in all of these realms. While not a replacement for work in the physical, it is a great help and not to be discarded as a method. I do most of this kind of thing in the two temples I mentioned when speaking of the Watchtower above.

18   Expect to be asked to help spirits in these realms at times. I often find that I spend a few minutes sort of cleaning up things, or helping stuck entities get unstuck.

19   Expect this to be weird. As you get comfortable with being in the Otherworld, things can shift pretty radically. People also experience for the most part things that fit their aesthetic sensibilities. Most of the faces or visuals we find there are generated by us, as a way of making sense of what we experience. Sometimes we will meet a being that looks very human. Over time, this may change into something distinctly non-human. Remember, the Otherworld is indeed *other!*

The following are two entries from my journal which may help to clarify much of what I have spoken to above.

Christmas Eve. I induced, then settled in layers. Into darkness. Into space. I then noticed that there was a "layer" that was like a second energetic self, and that my consciousness "nestled" in that second self. I began to "raise" the second self above the first, an inch at a time, an inch with each breath. I rose it up 4–6 inches, and fully situated my consciousness into it. I became aware that there were billions of connections between this second self and my body. They were deeply enmeshed and attached. I "flipped" myself over in the second self, so I was directly above, connected to, and looking down at the first self. I began to scan the first self for energy leaks, and closed them. I scanned for luminous fibers, and removed them. I scanned the whole body and healed any illness or dis-ease I found. I fed the first self with the power of the Field, which the second self was more clearly aware of. I gently built an egg-like shield of grey mist to protect the selves from interference and harm. This shell would also repel unwanted advances and attachments from luminous fibers. I deepened everything. I was/became aware of how I was nestled among a billion billion spirit beings who are similarly enmeshed. I performed the invocations from the second self onto the first and let it grow and adapt to the moment, I blessed my body, and the first self, and settled into a deeper knowledge of how I exist and function within the Field, how I am nestled in the flow of fate, a sailor on its seas. My ship strong and swift and deep of keel, always moving towards the currents of power that serve me best. I then shifted to the knowledge that I am the world tree, and followed my roots deep into the core of the earth and my branches far into the heavens above. I became more aware of how fully enmeshed I am in all three worlds. I then became aware of how I am the crossroads, the nexus of the six ways, the point of the weaving of Wyrd, how I am the pathfinder, how I am the beautiful connections and reality of the Field. This is.

This entry is from a few days later.

It took longer to relax, so I played with the words as I went along.

"I breathe and notice that my feet have relaxed completely, and are quiet and calm."

"I notice that I am very still and quiet. Very still, and very quiet. I start slipping into silence."

That kind of thing.

Once in, I move my consciousness to the second self. I settle it in the heart, and spend time there, enjoying the quiet. In time I raise the second self, and as usual I flip my perspective so I am looking down at my body. I do my healing work, singing closed any energy leaks, and removing a few stubborn attachments. I name those that I know. In time, that work seems done, and I become aware that I am at the crossroads, facing the Northern Mountain. I "sit" above my body, whose feet are in the North and whose head is in the South. I begin to do the hand work that the Night Mother taught me. The second self looks at its hands and sees them as the raven's talons, strong and deft. The raven hops free, and flies a big circle around us before settling back beside us on the left. We look at our hands again, and they shift into the wolf's paws, wide and warm, sensitive. The wolf slips free and circles us, then settles on the right side. We look at our hands, and they narrow a touch, and the Faerie is there. He is a bit taller and narrower than my body, with larger eyes. He is very still. He settles behind my body, and my head is in his lap, his left hand on my forehead and his right along my neck and jaw. His stillness settles through us. From the vision of the second self, I see that he holds both the head of my body as it is now, and as it will be, a simple skull. This is comforting. We sit, and I do my invocations, and when they are complete, the other selves slip back into the second self in the order they emerged, raven, wolf, Faerie. As they settle in I can feel them more clearly in me than ever, solid, watchful, comforting. We gaze awhile at the Northern Mountain, and then embrace our body and merge back into it completely, flipping our perception back to the front. Our consciousness sits solidly in our heart, and I return fully to the wake-world.

CHAPTER THIRTEEN

SIMPLE DIVINATION: THE PENDULUM

Divination is not a major part of my work, if we are speaking of using tools. I know many who do their best work through the continuous reading of cards, bones, runes, and the like. This has never been my way. I tend to get most of the answers to the questions I have by less mechanical means, during meditation, trance, or dreams.

Divination is, however, extraordinarily useful in two particular ways or circumstances. The first is when you need or desire information that is not readily available by other means. Then you can turn to your tool of choice, be they tea leaves, tarot cards, or the I Ching, and see if they are able to provide (and you are able to interpret!) the answers you hope for. The second is as a tool to increase options. When we choose to divine for options, that for me is something special. Divination is one of the ways of asking the Field "*how can I get from where I am to where I desire to be?*" This second path is where I tend to go, to get help in pointing out my blind spots.

When I need or want to clarify something, be it a good direction to move in or to find a block or intrusion, in most cases this leads me to the pendulum.

The pendulum is a good tool in that it can be fashioned on the spot (I've used a strand of hair and a nail before) and has a basically nonexistent learning curve.

Anything with a bit of weight that can be attached to a single string or thread can work as a pendulum. Rings tied to thread can work very well. Mine is a hand-turned beauty of a brass pocket plumb bob made by Richard Kell in England. After twenty-five years of use, it's a lively creature! It lights up visually when I use it.

The method with a pendulum is question and answer. And like any other form of divination, the quality of the question is everything. Be specific and rigorous in the formation of your question. For the pendulum, which is pretty much a yes/no process, this means that asking "*will I get what I am asking for if I do ___ ritual?*" will yield useable results whereas "*should I do ritual?"* will not.

As the pendulum is a yes-no (for the most part) tool, we have to form questions that can be answered yes or no! So care in formulating our questions, and being willing to ask a *lot* of them is the key.

I suggest Camelia Elias' book *Marseille Tarot: Towards the Art of Reading* for a good approach to questions in divination. It is also the best source I have found for reading tarot for those it doesn't usually work well for, like me.[1]

You can find very complex pendulum charts, but I use a simple one, as shown.

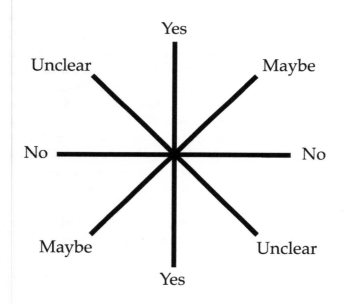

A SIMPLE PENDULUM MAP

---

1   Camelia Elias' book *Marseille Tarot: Towards the Art of Reading* and the Jean Noblet Marseille Tarot deck as reconstructed by Jean Claude Flornoy are my tarot mainstays, and are brutally honest and reliable for more complex divination. I also find the Noblet deck has a good sense of humor!

You can draw out a diagram like the one on the facing page to start. In time you will know the meaning of all the swings implicitly, and won't need a chart. You just hold the pendulum so it hangs freely over the center of the diagram, and begin working with it. Ask the pendulum: "Can you show me a *yes* to calibrate?" And continue through the directions. I always repeat this process before I read. Don't help! Let it sit still, spin, change directions. Talk to it: "I have no idea what you are doing! Can you give me a *yes* again?" I recall it taking some time for us to get onto the same page when I first began.

As you proceed, you can ask for "clearer" swings. As long as the direction is clear, you are good.

Here is an example of how I approach this. My questions are in normal text, the responses in parenthesis:

> *Hi pendulum, I'd like to chat about a few things. Can I get a "yes" to calibrate?* (no swing)
> *Can I really get a yes?* (YES)
> *Excellent, thank you! Can I get a no?* (NO)
> *Beautiful, thank you.* (pendulum is still)
> *L. has asked me to do some protection work for her. Is this something I can effectively help her with?* (half-assed YES)
> *Clarify that, please.* (strong YES)
> OK. *I am thinking of building a protection talisman for her. I am tending towards something using Archangel Michael. Will this be suitable and effective for her?* (NO)
> OK. *How about something linked to Freya?* (strong YES)
> *Should I involve any other deities or spirits in this working?* (NO)
> OK. *Thank you...*

Obviously I could continue on, but I think the process should be quite clear. With the pendulum, keep it simple, yes or no, and feel free to rephrase, circle back, and take your time. Be careful that you are not asking two questions at the same time! Recalibrate any time you feel the need to, and ask for stronger swings.

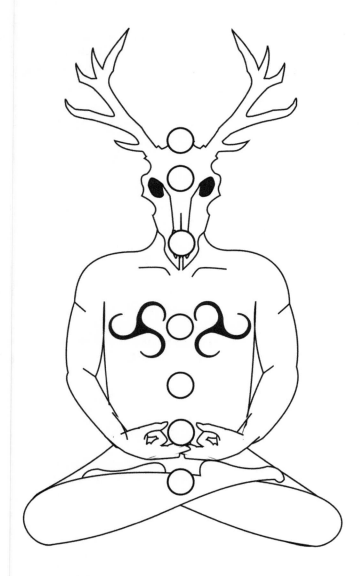

LOCATION OF CHAKRAS FOR VOWEL TONING

CHAPTER FOURTEEN

RAISING POWER AND FINDING A MAGICAL VOICE

"Raising power" here refers to generating or directing magical energy, a kind of energetic or psychic charge, to add life to a working or spell. It also helps to clear energy channels in the body that can become blocked in day to day life. The Fire Snakes practice is a method of raising power. Raising power also aids the processes that lead to being able to shift the point of conception of the self.

There are two main ways of doing this. The first is to work up a sweat, increase the heart rate, and more or less speed up your psychical vibrations. The second is the reverse. To slow down, become quiet and calm, slow the heart rate, and relax deeply. The first method is sometimes called "excitatory" and the second method "inhibitory."

These methods, like most aspects of this work, tend to bleed into each other. The root of either is a shift of "normal" consciousness to one more conducive to the work at hand.

The obvious excitatory methods are drumming, dance, hard physical exercise, and sex, basically things that lead to exhaustion.

The inhibitory methods are more in the relaxation, sensory deprivation, meditation, and trance end of things. This is where I tend to work personally.

One of the easier methods of raising power has to do with the magical voice.

This first practice came to me (in a different form) from Peter J. Carroll,[1] and I find it incredibly useful. It has counterparts in the use of mantra, chants, and also in *galdr*, or rune-singing. You can find many variants of it if you look into chakra toning.

The process is simple. You sit, relax, and breathe. Then you begin "vibrating" the seven (this is somewhat arbitrary, as I learned with five) vowels, focusing your attention on each of the seven related points along

---

1   As part of his Gnostic Pentagram Ritual. Peter J. Carroll, *Liber Kaos*.

the centerline of the body, generally referred to as chakras. In time, you will be able to sense the vibration of each tone in the desired area. Work your way up and back down a few times. When you are ready to stop, bring the attention to the belly point, and consciously choose to store any excess energy there.

The sounds rise in pitch as you climb from root to crown.

The first chakra or root sound is UUH (as in "up"), low and guttural.

The second chakra, at the sacrum or base of the spine, a few fingers below your navel is OOO (as in "too").

The third chakra is OH (as in "no").

The fourth chakra, at the heart, is AH (as in "saw").

The fifth chakra, at the throat, is EYE (as in sky).

The sixth chakra, at the third eye, between the brows, is AY (as in "stay").

The seventh chakra, at the crown of the head, is EEE (as in "see"), as high as you can comfortably go.

We can use these sounds, once we have opened up our voice to them, in many ways. We can use them to "set" our consciousness in a particular location or vibration. For example, if I am feeling muddled in my thoughts or tired, I can sing into the higher points to clear my head, or vibrate Tibetan monk–style low and guttural to generate more energy in the lower chakras and root my energy to the ground.

I can bring these tones into my evocations and invocations, again, to draw particular powers into the work. This is done via feel, in my case.

For the most part, as I am by nature fairly head-centric, I get the most mileage from going low and getting more of my guts involved.

Try playing with your name. See if you can speak it from each point in turn, from the rumbling lows to the highest highs. Try this with the names of your deities, spirits, or angels if you work with them. How does Hekate or Ganesha or Michael feel to you when "called" from the different points or chakras?[2]

What seems to be the nature of each vowel sound? Does each seem

---

2   In other words, does it feel and work the same when you call Hekate from the throat chakra, using that pitch (and precision is not key here, trust me!) as when you call her from the root chakra, using that deep deep pitch?

truly different, and is the difference one of quality, of shading, or outright color?

Pick a word of Power. We can use a rune (this is a form of *galdr*[3]), perhaps "Algiz" or something else that is of interest. Speak it from each point, and see if you find that it has "a happy place," a particular point that it resonates with, that gets it really humming.

Drop the volume, and tone it quietly, or crank it up and set the walls to vibrate. Pretend you are a monster and speak it in your monster voice. Pretend you are a Tuvan throat singer or Tibetan monk. Play around to find which voices work well for you, which voices carry particular powers within them.

These practices open up energy channels, both bodily and psychic. They help to clear out blockages and gunk that can clog our senses and our abilities to manifest. You may get some weird side effects, memories of old events or dreams that have been held in the body when working this practice. You may find you can release trapped, old emotions that have been stuck in a particular "voice" that you had stopped using at some time in the past.

A LAST EXERCISE ON VOICE

One morning, decide on a word of power you would like to manifest, but do not say it aloud, not even in a whisper. Carry it inside you all day, in your body, somewhere near your center. Bring your attention to it over and over, dozens of times, while you go about your day. But keep it secret, keep it safe. When evening comes, and you can be alone and uninterrupted, take your word, still kept quietly near the center of your body, to the altar. Sit, light a candle, and begin to vibrate the vowel tones. Run the vowels a few times, up, down, back up. Once you feel nice and strong and open, begin to notice once more the word you hold in your center. Begin to quietly hum the vowel tones with your mouth closed. Let the word you have held all day know that it is almost time to be free. Feel its desire for freedom, to be birthed from your lips into the Field. Let it rise from root to crown with your humming of the tones, and after the last, highest "EEE"

---

3   Galdr is a form of runic spell work, often called "rune-singing."

(or at another point if that makes gut-sense), open your mouth and speak the word. This is a peculiarly potent practice, so choose your word well!

CHAPTER FIFTEEN

OFFERINGS

Falling in love is driven by many things, chemistry being a big one, but mind, soul, spirit, fascination, respect, desire all blend together to create a particular effect, that of focusing our attention on another. We look to the other, we note their posture, scent, curve of muscle and bone. We strive to understand their emotional state and the movement of their thoughts. These things are endlessly fascinating. We tend to deepen the bond via offerings. We offer them food, bring them coffee, and see if there is something they would like us to do for them and then do it. This is not entirely altruistic. There is an implicit desire for reciprocation in all of these actions. A hope that what we give will bring happiness or ease to the other, and that this will allow us to remain in their presence, and perhaps deepen the relationship.

This is a good perspective to take on making spirit offerings as well.

Much like bringing your guy chocolates, we bring the Spirits and Powers offerings with the intention to make them happy, and with luck, have them look more favorably upon us.

My go-to offerings are water, candles, and incense, and various kinds of food.

Cool water is the most basic of offerings. I offer water to pretty much all of the spirits I work with. Water will on occasion be "fixed up" for spirits I think or know would like it by adding a bit of crushed dried rose petals or a touch of certain perfumes. I have relations with spirits who respond well to particular tinctures or to drops of particular oils added the water. These kinds of additions are best worked out on a one-on-one basis.

I am very basic with candles, using almost nothing but tea lights and Shabbat candles. They don't have to be fancy, as we will make them fancy by dressing them.

For incenses, I tend to use resin incense on an incense heater, which allows a much more controlled release of scent without burning. It is also far more economical as a small amount of resin can be heated for hours, rather than minutes on a charcoal.

Some spirits I have worked with also like tea, coffee, and some like milk. I think the best way to proceed is by following the hints the spirits give and then seeing what happens. Some spirits are decidedly into alcohol and tobacco, some find these offensive. If you like, you can sit with the pendulum or cards and ask questions as to what might be a good offering.

I think the most direct way to think of offerings is as offering nourishment or food. Sometimes this is outright food, and many I know who bake, bake for the spirits. I tend to give offerings of unbroken eggs, tortillas, chili sauce, fruit, flowers.

It is good to consider candles as food for the spirits as well. Candles are a solid energy source (wax, but this is also true of oil in oil lamps or even wood for a fire) that is largely consumed by burning. As it is consumed, it is transformed from solid matter into heat, smoke, ash, and carbon. This transmutation allows the spirits and powers to feed on these energies and their subtle natures.

We can "dress" a candle, a term that means to consecrate, usually with herbs, powders, oils, and for some, glitter (glitter can be a big thing, although I am not a user!). We do this to make the candle more special. We might inscribe a petition or sigil on it, oil it up, and rub or roll it in the powders, herbs, what have you.[1] For tea lights and novena candles that I burn in glass, I add these things by sprinkling them on top. Remember that candles start fires, and too much *materia* on top of a candle can ignite as another wick. Be smart!

Dressing the candle is like making a meal more interesting, in that we add delectable "spices," in the hopes of creating something truly delicious and attractive. As we are feeding our friends and allies, this is a good thought-habit to get into as we work.

---

1   As with many things in magic, you can and may come across many and contradictory "rules" about how you dress a candle. These may or may not have any bearing on how you do things! I remain, always, with a "go with your gut" approach unless something actively shows me to do it another way. Do what seems good to you!

Here is one way to get started with making offerings, heavily influenced by Jason Miller.[2]

Step one is being polite to those you wish to interact with. It is polite to light a candle, a stick of incense, and offer a cup or bowl of cool water. Quiet your mind. Then once you have chilled yourself out, speak. Here's an example:

> *Spirits who aid and guard me, be with me now and always. Please feed on this light, smoke, and water. Be nourished and strengthened. Spirits who obstruct my path, spirits that I have offended by ignorance or transgression, please feed on this light, smoke, and water. Be nourished and strengthened. Let there be peace between us for all of our days.*

Sit, be quiet for a while. If you feel agitated, get yourself calm again.

Now is a good time to talk about what you are trying to do, trying to achieve, trying to improve in your life. Ask the spirits who aid and guard you for their help. Do not demand or beg, just ask. Think about a time when someone asked you for something in a way that made it a joy to give it to them. Try to bring that spirit to the process. Here is an example:

> *Spirits who watch over me, aid and guide me on my path. Open the roads that I travel so that they may be free of obstacles. Grant me clear vision so that I can see the ways forward. Protect me from all harm and from all wrathful beings who would do me harm.*

If you do the above regularly, you will cultivate a relationship with spirits already aligned to you and your life. In time you may find that making offerings and then asking for assistance will be most of the magical "working" that you need to do.

HEATING AND COOLING

This concept is present in a variety of African magical traditions. It can be viewed molecularly for ease. Heat is generated by, and itself generates, a

---

2   Jason Miller, *The Sorcerer's Secrets: Strategies to Practical Magick* and also in his Strategic Sorcery course.

faster movement of the elements involved. Cold does the reverse, slowing things down.

We can use these facts and ideas in our magical work easily. If I am making an offering to a spirit I wish to become more active, I can give it hot things: peppers, coffee, ginger, tobacco, most hard alcohol, red and black items.

If I wish to calm a spirit down, to quiet things down, I offer cool water, cool fruit, flowers, cool colors.

In practice, I give all of the spirits I work with cool water. When I am doing more active work with one or a group in particular, I give them coffee as well. Some of the spirits that like things spicy are very fond of coffee with sugar, cayenne pepper, and cinnamon.

The practice of making offerings is perhaps the most frequently ignored aspect of sorcerous practice. There is a tendency to be demanding, to ask and never give in return. This is both rude and inefficient. The regular giving of offerings does more to "grease the wheels of fate" than any other practice I know.

CHAPTER SIXTEEN

FOR THE DEAD

We are all born of someone. This is. Be they saints or sadists or somewhere in-between, we are links in a long, long chain of lives. We may want nothing to do with many of the links to which we are directly attached, and I'm the last person to tell you that you need to connect any more deeply with those who have done you harm. I myself skip some links in the chain when it comes to working with the ancestors and the dead.

In some ways, the ancestors are the closest of Spirits to us. Due to their previous experience as people much like us, and due to our all being part of the vast chain of humanity, they understand us in some ways better than the less human Others.

I feed my familial dead by making offerings to them. This is the simplest of offerings. Cool water in a clear glass, a plain white cloth, and a small white plate for offerings. A white votive candle in a clear glass. Once a week I offer fresh water, a candle, and a bit of frankincense. I thank them for their aid, their protection, and their interest in my life and work. I ask those of the dead that do not understand my work to accept that it is done for the good of all, even though my ways are not theirs, and to support my work even without understanding it or agreeing with it.[1]

I deal with the more general dead in a few ways. They are all fed in my daily offerings at the altar, I visit with them while traveling, and I sometimes aid the recent dead in getting "unstuck" in the spaces between the life of the flesh and where they travel to once it is done. In this way, I am working with the overall field of the dead that may not have specific blood ties to me. Some of these dead are of particular spiritual "lines," some are not.

---

1 Thanks to Andrew McGregor of the Hermit's Lamp in Toronto for suggesting this practice, which came out of a recent reading. It has been a great help.

These practices can be disturbing to some and it wise to remember: we are all here due to the dead who came before us. The very nutrients in the soil where we grow the food we eat are created by the processes of death and decay. Even to clear a field to grow grains or beans destroys a vast number of lifeforms inhospitable to the process of farming. There is no life without dying. There is no birth without death. We came here to die, as reads my brother's tattoo.

From my perspective as a sorcerer, it is clear that death is decidedly not the end of our time in the Field. I've seen clear manifestations of ghosts, been visited by and have visited both of my grandmothers, and met a goodly number of the lost and wandering dead. Are all of these things "real"? From a magical sense, absolutely. And as this is a book on magic, that is all that really matters.

Practically I suggest including the dead in your magical practice, and the way I mentioned above seems sound to me; the familial dead get their own simple or elaborate altar and offerings, and the more general, or "Mighty Dead" as they are sometimes called, get worked into your general spirit offerings. Should you be called to separate the general dead further, do so and see what comes of it. We all develop our own ways. Try making basic offerings to both classes once a month at the very least, and once a week is probably better. Remember that in most cases this type of offering is the work of a few minutes, although some will choose or be guided to far more involved and time-consuming practices.

CHAPTER SEVENTEEN

PETITIONS

Petitions are a simple way to ask for help from spirits or to focus intentions in sorcery. I'll show you how I learned to make them.

Take a smallish square of paper, and write out what you are asking for (your petition). In this example, I am asking St. Michael for protection. I write my petition over and over from top to bottom. Some people insist that the pen must not be lifted from the page, however, I don't find that it matters too much. Do what seems good to you!

Here's the first step:

> *St. Michael watch over me and protect*
> *me from all harm St. Michael watch over*
> *me and protect me from all harm St.*
> *Michael watch over me and protect me*
> *from all harm St. Michael watch over me*
> *and protect me from all harm St.*
> *Michael watch over me and protect me*
> *from all harm St. Michael watch over me*
> *and protect me from all harm St.*
> *Michael watch over me and protect me*
> *from all harm St. Michael watch over me*
> *and protect me from all harm*

Now turn the paper a quarter turn and write your petition out again, over the top of what you just wrote. Do this four times in total, so that you have written your petition four times. It should be mostly unreadable now.

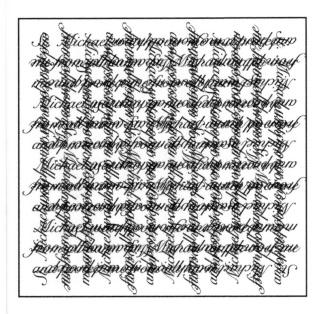

Now start again, still writing over the top, writing your name or the name of the person you are doing the petition for. Write it over and over to fill the page, then turn the page a quarter, just like the original petition. Again, write the name over the entire sheet four times in total. It will obviously turn into even more of an unreadable mess, so there is no need to show all the steps.

Once you have finished the writing, you (as always!) make it special. You can spit on it to link it to you, add oils and herbs or powders and perfumes that make sense, or pray over it.

The usual next step is to fold or roll it up. This is straightforward. Roll or fold it towards you for things you want to bring into your life, and away from you for things you are sending away.

You can be done at this point, or perhaps the petition will go onto an altar, into a vessel or container, or into a wallet (for drawing money perhaps, or simply to keep it close). Do whatever makes sense to you, as in the end, you are the final arbiter of magical logic.

CHAPTER EIGHTEEN

SIGILS, SERVITORS & SPIRITS

Sigil magic is a foundational practice, and in many ways, it is hard to beat for efficiency and effectiveness. There is nothing to believe (and so nothing to resist), it bypasses the internal censors by design, and can be done essentially anywhere with nothing more than a pen and a scrap of paper or a finger in the dirt.

Sigils can be thought of as a method of coding information into a dense packet that can be gently slipped into our deep mind. From there it is free to interact with the Field without hindrance from our waking selves, and what I learned of by the name "the psychic censor."[1]

The psychic censor is that part of us that determines for better or worse what is possible for us. It is rarely for the better. The psychic censor mainly wishes to maintain things as they are. Unfortunately, things are not generally how we want them to be, or at least not as good as we believe they could be, or we would not be doing magic to change them! In practical terms, the psychic censor's function is to reduce the possibility of change.

Sigils bypass the psychic censor (and I keep naming it for a reason: it is important to keep sight of it in the early stages of this work, as it *is* working even when we are not aware of it) by turning our strong desires into images that are a) essentially meaningless to the rational mind (where the censor dwells) while b) being absolutely laden with meaning and intention in a form accessible to and easily assimilated by the deep mind.

The process is incredibly simple. This is one of those cases where if it seems complex, you are overcomplicating it!

Choose what change you are seeking to make, or what desire you would manifest in yourself or the world at large. If it is a complex series of things, break it down into discrete pieces.

Write down your intention, here are a few guidelines:

---

1   A reminder that I do not use this in the "ESP" related sense here, but in the original sense. From the Ancient Greek ψυχικός, *psukhikos*, "relative to the soul, spirit, mind."

Use positive language only. No negatives. I am unsure exactly why this is so, but after gods know how many hundreds or thousands of sigils I have done, this is clearly the case. So if, for example, you wanted to make a sigil for "Stop my ex-boyfriend Jimmy from stalking me," you will have much better success with "Jimmy fell in love with a guy from Florida and moved there with him."[2] Likewise, making sigils for becoming wealthy (or at least having enough to get by) work far better than those to "stop being broke."

Here are two examples of good language for sigils:

I am proceeding with my plans to move. (This is fair.)
I am moving. (This is better.)
I love where I have moved to. (This is best, as it is the completion of all of the above, and the deep mind will work with the Field to make it true.)

Or:

Stop me from eating junk food. (This sucks. Going into a coma would work.)
I am free of my addiction for sugary treats. (This is pretty good.)
I love eating only tasty food that is good for me. (This is killer. Again, it is the completion of all of the above, while completely avoiding issues of deprivation or loss.)

All these forms can work, with the better language always reflecting the positive *outcome* of the desired action or change.

I will use "I love where I have moved to" as our example. As you proceed from this point, try to gently not think about your intention-sentence. Try to view it as only letters becoming an image-creature, and so it will remain from here on out.

First, remove all repeated letters.

ILOVEWHRAMDT

2 Getting Jimmy to leave town because he really wanted to (whatever the reason – new guy, new job) is pretty much the gold standard in this kind of situation, making it have nothing to do with you. Even if you really hate the bastard.

If still too long, remove vowels, unless you really like them.

ILVWHRMDT

I then remove all letters that are mirrors or inversions or clearly contained in other letters. This is subjective and optional.

WHRDT

This is a good place for me, not too complex.

Now make a picture with these letters. Stack them, overlay them, reverse them, twist them. Turn them into an image that does not reflect your intention, a simple graphic or monogram.[3]

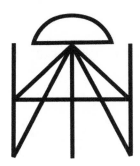

A SIMPLE, UNEMBELLISHED SIGIL

This is your sigil. I suggest it should be thought of as a Seed. I tend to make them as pretty as I can, embellishing them in any way that seems good to me. I try to get as "lost" in the whole process as I can. This essentially plants the "Seed" as I am creating it.

---

3   After making sigils for myself and others for thirty-plus years, just last week I discovered (hiding in a blind spot the size of a small country!) that I really love to make sigils with cursive letters. I suggest you give it a try!

SIGIL, EMBELISHED

Once the sigil is drawn and seems "cooked" or feels right, take a few moments getting quiet and centered. Then focus on the lines, the image, see if you can become a bit fascinated with it. Lower lighting or candle lighting is good. Let it shift in your vision. Perhaps it will actually "light up" or shift for a moment.

SIGIL FROM THE SAME WORDS, RENDERED IN CURSIVE

From this point very gently strive to only see it as a sigil, not related to any other thing. It is an image, a creature, a friend, but it is otherwise meaningless.

It can be helpful to do a few sigils at the same time. I tend to do three to twelve sigils at a time. This is known as "Shoaling" and if done well, I very quickly can't remember which sigil is which within the Shoal.[4]

As there is no way to "undo" a sigil, be smart about what you create them for.

I think of this approach like driving a ship. You can't un-travel the sea you have already traveled, so instead you change course as needed. In this case, you change course by using more sigils, and this is how you "steer" towards your intentions in sigil magic.

I expect that everyone comes to develop a best practice for themselves in this work. For me, I like to run with an overarching destination sigil and then steer with more specific sigils as I proceed.[5] You will see this reflected in other methods of working I suggest as well.

I used to use all sorts of methods to "charge" sigils. Here is what I do now and what works the best for me. I draw all of my sigils on three inch squares of thick black paper with silver ink, or thick white paper with black ink. When it is time to "activate" or charge them, I light a candle on a table in a darkened room and mix up all of the sigils in the shoal I am working with, like shuffling cards. I call on the spirits who aid and guard me to be present and assist me. I begin laying out the sigil "cards" in a sort of grid pattern, and gaze on each as I turn it over until it "shifts." This shifting can be subtle or extreme – it doesn't seem to make a difference, it's just momentary sense of movement. Then I lay down the next sigil, and repeat. There is no need for any kind of tension. If nothing shifts, just move on to the next card. If only certain sigils shift, that's fine as well. Remember that we are seeding the sigils into the deep mind, and this is a gentle, easy process. I lay out the entire shoal, and gaze at that as a whole. If I have room, I often leave the shoal out for the day, where I can see it, and then repeat the entire process the next day, shuffling the shoal, laying it out, and so on. I remove sigils from the shoal when they seem "done." As I don't know what

---

4   Gordon White, *The Chaos Protocols: Magical Techniques for Navigating the New Economic Reality.*

5   An example. Let's say that I am working on boosting my skills at divination or oracular work. I may create a sort of over-arching sigil: "I divine clearly and consistently." Then I may add other sigils to guide this: "The Tarot Trumps speak to me directly and accurately" and "I frame questions for my readings clearly and concisely" etc., etc.

each sigil is for, this is another case of letting the deep mind be the driver. When I remove a sigil from the shoal, I tend to burn it.

Another approach using sigils is to create what is called a servitor. You start with a sigil that represents something you would regularly do magic for. For example, in the early 90's when obscure magical texts were harder to find than now, I had one that hunted books for me.

To use a sigil for servitor creation, you focus on tasks rather than outcome.

For example, if you were a male of a certain age, you might do a sigil for GET LAID. Trust me, you would. Whereas if you got smarter after playing with this for a while you might create a servitor whose function was "MAKE ME AWARE OF PEOPLE INTERESTED IN HAVING SEX WITH ME." This is actually *way* more useful, as if it does its job, then you get to decide what to do with that information. It also removes a lot of the potential weirdness of how things manifest. Which is potentially very, very weirdly![6]

Now here is where I break with a lot of chaos magicians. Servitor work led me to my current approach to magic. I now don't think we actually "make" a servitor most of the time.[7] I instead believe that we attract spirits who gain benefit from working with us, who choose to fill an open employment position. They usually desire something in return. This is not a problem! You can often decide what that is: "I'll give you an egg and three red candles a week, and energetic offerings. And special treats (bonuses) for particularly stellar performances." This is symbiosis.

There is an old dream I had from when I was in my early twenties. In the dream, I am watching two beings looking over a book. It is an obviously ancient grimoire, huge and ornate, like something from a movie. I cannot see the pages at first, as I am above and behind the beings. They move apart enough that I can see the pages, which are full of drawings. Some of the drawings are of my tattoos, some are of my friend's ink. I am somehow

---

6   One of the best arguments for a spirit world in my opinion is exactly how truly peculiarly magical results can manifest. It's sort of stunning, and seems to show both consciousness and a twisted sense of humor at times.

7   This is not the same as "never."

told that yes, this is a book of spirits. And that these beings use these sigils to contact and call upon us (the book spirits) to aid them.

The story as the spirits told it is that we are more than we think we are, we both live our life as we are aware of it, and at least some of us function to the Others as they function to us.

Do you see why I think this symbiosis thing is good to strive for? And why I think being polite is wise?

Let's continue. So we do the work to create a servitor. We sigilize the function, whatever that is. My book-finding servitor was generated from the word "bookfinder." We create a sigil, and then we create a house for it, a material base. Perhaps we paint the sigil on a stone, crystal, box, poppet, or bone. We can also simply create the sigil on paper, and place it in a vessel or jar.[8] This is definitely a good thing to turn into an art project! We feed it with power to bring it into being. This feeding can take many forms. We can run the Orbits or Fire Snakes practice and feed it raw energy. We can perform a more involved evocation if we like, calling to the servitor to inhabit the material base. We can make offerings of food, candles, incense – all the usual methods, with the goal of bringing the servitor to life. When we feel like we have achieved this (and this may take a few tries, there's no rules about how long it takes to "wake up" your servitor!), we ever after treat the servitor as an at least semi-sentient spirit being.

So now we have a sigil, energy source, and body (the material base is always a body by function even if not a body in an animal sense). We name it, hopefully something that makes sense in the moment, that sparks something. And now we have a new friend and/or helper. There is one main thing to watch out for: servitors are a bit like working dogs. Trouble comes if they are mistreated or don't have a job to do. So it is important (seriously, really important) to give them a job. When they do a good job, they get treats, when they are less successful we try and figure out why and adjust.

Why magic "doesn't work" can be a tricky question, and with servitors it can be more so than usual. Which makes it a useful practice in and of itself. We need to weed out obvious issues: What was the function it was made for? Are we asking it to work outside of that function? Are we getting messages that we don't like and so don't recognize?

8   There is quite a lot more on this later on in the chapter called "Vessels."

This can be pretty obvious but also somehow invisible at the same time. Maybe I made the servitor to help me be aware of who might like to have sex with me. And maybe that is happening, but I am not noticing because there are actually other criteria on my end that I didn't explain. Maybe I am not interested in women. Or people who smoke, or drunks. Or maybe I have upper and lower age limits, or I'd like to actually be able to talk to this person about sports or politics or magic. These servitor-creatures, whatever they really are, reified thought-forms or spirits we have attracted, are usually very open to training or adjustment of focus. You go back to the altar (or wherever the material base is) and make offerings. Thank it for whatever it has done so far. Explain that you are not getting what you were hoping for. Listen (i.e., pay attention to sense impressions, do some divination). Then clarify: "Look, I am interested in straight or bi women who are within say ten years of my age who like to take psychedelics, watch Star Trek, and fuck while listening to death metal, and who would like to do these things with me." Now you might actually get some real action. You have radically narrowed the field, so you will need to put yourself in places where these things are more likely. Maybe wear your Star Trek pin to death metal shows.

All of these ideas point you in the direction you are looking to go. They all clarify your intentions. They all work on multiple levels. None of them individually is absurd and improbable. All of this is obvious and all of it is often ignored by otherwise intelligent people (myself included).

So now you have set up both you and your servitor for success. You have also created an environment where you both can learn together.

Then the inevitable happens: you are out watching Grievous Angel sing songs about Satan and your servitor says, "go to the upstairs bar, NOW."[9] And you aren't going to be stupid and second guess this, right? Because you have done all this work so that this will happen, right? So you don't ask why, you just go to the upstairs bar. And you see her right away: Watain shirt and a Star Trek patch on her vest. You go up and politely smile and say, "I love Watain, and that patch is rad." And with any luck or social

---

9   This may actually happen this way. I have had servitors give me explicit instructions: "Turn left, now. The guy on the right behind you is going to mug you if you stay on this street." More likely, you'll get a seemingly random urge, a hint. Learning to pay attention to these sometimes vague messages is a big part of effective magic.

skills, you will soon be on your way to a blissed-out future of detuned guitars and acid-fueled sex.

So what do you do with your servitor now? Remember, your out-of-work helper spirit will eventually get into all sorts of trouble. This is nearly inevitable.

My approach is to see if it would like another job to focus its attentions on. Maybe it could now help you find a better job so you can buy your girl nice death-metal trinkets. Usually, they do want another job. You just work the process. Ask questions, listen (or do divination if that is your thing), and talk about what the next project is.

Which leads back to the "did you make it, or did it answer your call?" question.

If you made it out of the statement "MAKE ME AWARE OF PEOPLE IN-TERESTED IN HAVING SEX WITH ME," how does that change into "HELP ME SEE OPTIONS FOR MORE ENTERTAINING AND LUCRATIVE EMPLOY-MENT"?

It may seem a little like asking your car to turn into a dishwasher. But it isn't, somehow. In most cases the shift will be very smooth. Keep up with the offerings, keep giving bonuses for good work. And what you may find is that you don't really need very many of these helper-friends. What happened for me is that I mostly stopped making them. I just started asking whoever was around to help.[10]

One last bit. If you decide to be done with your servitor, politely release it, thanking it for its good work, and in some way un-make or scatter its material base. I've burned them, cast them into the ocean, broken material bases into pieces, etc. Just finish up the relationship cleanly and clearly. Ghosting your servitors is not a good idea!

10 I can't really suggest this as a general best practice and it is almost certainly not the best place to start, it's just how I work now.

CHAPTER NINETEEN

TRAINING POWER

Part of the process of learning to work with these approaches is realizing that sentient or as-sentient entities (spirits, in other words) are much like the other people you meet. They have their natures, which rarely change, and rarely due to outside pressure. But like other people, they are often amenable to persuasion and enticement. This means that you can forge alliances and come to agreements with them.[1]

We can see this in the case of something like home protection. I "ward" the doors and windows to keep unhelpful spirits and energies from entering the house. One view is that I am asking the threshold-spirits, who are already present (due to the nature of the space: in-between spaces "house" in-between space entities) to simply take note of things which may not be their normal parameters of interest or behavior.

In this view a good deal of the work of magic begins to make a whole lot of not-very-esoteric sense. If doorways are thresholds, which they are, they are by definition liminal spaces. They are openings between worlds, to inside my house from outside, or to bedroom from kitchen. So I am literally moving between realms when I move from room to room. It seems logical to me that my doorways then hold space for liminal, threshold beings. How could they not? Otherwise it would be like asking the sea to not hold space for fish. So if I begin to ask my doors and doorways to keep my space "closed" to unhelpful influences when I leave, and then thank them for doing a good job when I return, this reinforces the second nature of a door: not only a way to enter into another space, but a gate or block to keep

---

[1] These alliances and agreements are at times perceived as "demonic pacts" by some who are unable to step outside of a dualistic mindset. Do you "forge a pact" with your plumber when he comes to fix the shower, or do you simply come to an agreement on a piece of work and its cost? It is usually unhelpful to try to use the definitions of things created by those who either do not believe in them, or see them as inherently evil or wrong.

some people or things outside.[2]

If I do not ask for this (which in a sense is what "warding" is: asking for protection, discretion, to prevent or exclude certain elements or beings from entry) how should my doors or windows know that I desire this? And how can I make this of interest to them? I do this via my attention, which is in itself an offering, and by more explicit offerings, like candles or incense or periodically washing the doors and thanking them for what a good job they do.

I can give two examples of mundane life that may help clarify how I think this works. In the first, I was living in a very rough neighborhood. I'd only been there a few days when I was expecting a visitor. I heard a person scream and some kind of altercation out on the street, and so I dropped off of my second-floor balcony, hunting knife in hand, to check it out (this is not really suggested, but it worked out!). Turns out this was something that happened all the time and was a domestic violence situation, not my expected visitor (which sucked as well, but was not an equation I could have any part in successfully). I ended up having a few cigarettes with the guys who "ran" the street, and then my friend showed up. After this, things changed. I was the crazy guy with the knife who ran towards trouble (in the neighbors' minds) and so was, therefore, interesting and perhaps useful. They in the future walked all my visitors to my door. This was cemented with the occasional cigarettes and beers from me to them.

Nothing about me or these guys changed. What changed was our relationship. I had clarified my point of view: my friends would not be harmed when visiting. I was cool to everyone. I cemented this with offerings (beer and cigarettes). I did my part (like not having seen certain people when certain other people asked if I had indeed seen them!). This approach works both in the human and spirit realms.

The second example is I worked in a bookstore on the night shift, from six to ten P.M. One night a guy came in and very politely asked if it was OK if he sold some (likely stolen) goods outside the store. I said sure, as long as he kept things mellow. He asked if I had a broom he could borrow. I gave him one, he swept the sidewalk out front and set up shop. This went on for weeks. We never became friends, but became closer.

---

2   In practice I do make regular offerings to the doors, windows, fences and gates on my property. I also explicitly thank all of my animals for the work they do every day.

One night this gentleman, we'll call him Maurice, had set up shop, after cleaning the front sidewalks as usual. A bit later a guy came into the shop and started messing with a woman who was shopping. This escalated a bit, and I walked him out of the store. About twenty minutes (and probably a few beers) later, he came moving very fast towards the store with his hand inside his jacket. I saw him approaching and sort of braced for impact, not knowing what was coming, when Maurice stepped in front of the door, said a few words to the guy, who looked into the shop and then took off. I asked Maurice a bit later what had happened. He said the guy had a knife in his coat and was looking to show me that I shouldn't disrespect him. Maurice told him "Man, he didn't disrespect you, you disrespected that woman. But if you go in there with that knife you're gonna meet the shotgun behind the counter, I can tell you that!" I said, "but Maurice, I don't have a shotgun!" Maurice laughed, "You do now, my friend, or at least everyone around here thinks you do!"

This kind of relationship is what I meant earlier about antibodies. By being clear, by making offerings based on that clarity, and by not countering that clarity by being a dick, or by bringing in unhelpful entities (which can also be humans!) into my home or space, this whole series of processes forms a gestalt that supports my intentions.

We can easily counter our own best intentions by not taking total responsibility for our actions. I may want a quiet life, but if I surround myself with loud, erratic people I am not likely to have one, even if I love them. A common example is that we may wish to be healthy, but eat foods that work against this.

Here are is an example that may help to clarify this, while being a useful skill.

WARDING YOUR HOME

Clean your house thoroughly. Open all the doors and windows while you do the floors, which are the most important part. Take the trash out through the back door if this is an available option. Once the house is clean, mix up a bucket of water and some vinegar, and add a pinch of salt. You can add a light tea of protection related herbs, such as rosemary, rue, and hyssop. Feel free to add a touch of perfume (Florida Water being fairly classic) or an oil. As you add each item to the bucket, explain to it what you would like it to do.

Water of life, bring your powers to bear to clean and guard the thresholds of this house. Vinegar, bring your powers to clear and guard to the thresholds of this house. Beautiful herbs, bring your powers to bear to protect this house.

Or something of the sort. Now take your bucket, and clean your windows and doors, again asking what you wish. *"Window, allow only helpful spirits and allies into this house, send away all harmful influences that seek ingress into this place."* Do this with all the windows and doors. Periodically "renew" this work with a touch of diluted protection tea, oil, or perfume (rue and hyssop in a base of alcohol is nice and not very messy). You can add to this whatever makes sense – perhaps the sign of the cross, or hanging appropriate herbs or charms at each opening into your house.

When you operate your windows or doors, thank them for their work, being clear what you are thanking them for. This is important. In modern terms, be proactive not reactive. Ask your door to protect your home when you leave, and thank it when you return!

We train ourselves as we train our house of spirits. By being clear to the others around us, we become more clear to ourselves. Expect feedback if you are doing this right! I've tried to bring people into my house and been given the red light, a pure sensory kick of "What the fuck do you think you are doing bringing *that* in here? On our watch? We don't think so!" I learned to listen to this the hard way. If we don't listen, if we say we want one thing and then act as if we want its opposite, we are in a sense short-circuiting the work we are doing. This is what total responsibility requires.

One last example that may help to make this totally clear. I have goats, and I have dogs whose job is to protect them, mainly from other dogs and coyotes (who are canines and so dogs, right?). So it is unwise (in the extreme) for me to allow outsider dogs onto my property. It's mixed messaging, and the other dog might decide it is fun to chase a goat. And get taken out by my dogs! My dogs are wards and spirits that protect the goats. If I allow some predators in (the other dogs) how are they to know who to protect the goats from? I can short circuit their programming by being lax, by muddying the waters.

Keep your house clean, and be clear that the "Welcome" on the welcome mat comes with conditions. And honor them.

CHAPTER TWENTY

AT THE CROSSROADS: A BRIEF NOTE ON ROLES

If you choose to work magic, you become active in the spirit world. This sounds like a no-brainer, but it's a concept with ramifications that I don't see mentioned often.

We are spirits. We are presently embodied, but this does not change that fact. As we work in particular types or forms of magic, we become a bit like that which we work with. If we do a lot of "liminal" or crossroads work, we may take on pieces of the "jobs" that happen there. We become beings (spirits) of the crossroads to an extent. We gain particular skills or talents through familiarity, through regular exposure. This is in the nature of contagion, that what was once in contact remains in some way connected. This can have positive or negative influences, depending on the specific context and specific players. As we experience particular things, they stick to us and shape us. We then in time reflect that back into the world. In other words, if you spend a lot of time with door-keeper spirits, you become in at least a small sense a door-keeper spirit. At least enough to be recognized as such at times.

I've heard this idea, usually in the negative sense, where people become "tainted" by exposure to some types of spirits or places. But perhaps a better word is "colored." Perhaps if fairy dust (for example) is like the pollen from a dandelion, then others note its glow on those who spend time in fairy rings. And so this person, colored by contact with the fey, becomes related to them in some small fashion.

This is a good reason to both spend time surrounded by the things you would like to be "colored" by, and in cleansing and clearing work to remove those things you'd rather not carry with you.

I believe this to be true. While there are many options of "Others" that one can choose to spend time and energy with, it makes sense to me to choose very, very wisely. I have known many practitioners who felt called to work with very harsh, hungry, aggressive, and violent spirits. It is not my place to make a value judgment on this. If you are not willing to do extensive work to control your selves (as there are parts of self that are more easily influenced and swayed by malevolent spirits than others) and manage your environmental hygiene, then stick with those beings that align very closely with your overall gestalt[1] to begin with.[2]

On a related note, it is important to remember: you are what you do. You come in time to reflect your repeated actions. What you do day in and day out is practice. When we talk about "developing a practice," what is meant is "taking control of our selves, our thoughts, and our actions in a conscious effort to change who we are by changing (or simply consciously deciding) what we do."

If we don't make this a conscious decision (to practice towards the state of being and doing that we desire), we tend to practice whatever our default state is. So we get better at manifesting that default state, for better or (more usually) worse.

You are what you do. So choose what you do carefully. Choose who you engage with. Choose what stories you tell yourself about why things are the way they are for you. Choose to believe that you can change what needs to be changed. Act from this position. Make it true.

---

1   Gestalt is here defined as: an organized whole that is perceived as more than the sum of its parts. Form, shape. In other words, hang out with those that suit your desired scene or outcome, human and otherwise.

2   This is actually perhaps the best argument for a fairly simple practice centered around trance work, sigils, offerings and things like candle spells (in other words, the types of thing I am suggesting in this book) rather than a more classical spirit-conjuring and compulsion approach. There actually are rather nasty spirits out there, and working with them can produce unpleasant side effects for some people. This is not much different to my mind than choosing to not spend time around angry drunks who like to fight.

CHAPTER TWENTY ONE

ON THE STACKING OF SKULLS

In a magical sense, an altar[1] can be and is many things. It can be a table or shelf where we work, a place where the houses of Spirits we work with reside, a work of art, a command console for our vessel.[2] As always, we follow the currents of power and construct our altars to serve that flow. As such, there is no hard and fast rule for how they are made, what they look like or what goes on them.

Part of my main altar is mounted on the wall above my work bench, as my jewelry practice is the focal point of my work. There is a bookcase off to the side that holds most of my *materia*, tools, candles, and the like, and a few spirits have their houses there. The "working focus" is a small area, where the actual candles are burned, sigils empowered, and petitions made.

Here are a few concepts that might be of interest to those who are new to this altar building thing.

I tend to view the altar as a type of organic machine or device, a collection of parts that work together as a whole to perform (or to aid me to perform) a particular task or series of tasks. So I tend to have a primary focal point, which establishes a particular goal and defines the overall function of the device. More commonly this is something that speaks to me of a space in-between "normal" reality and magical reality. As is said in some traditions of witchcraft, a place "neither here nor there" or "between the worlds." This is an artistic vision and will be totally personal. It should

---

1   It is worth mentioning that an altar is most commonly a table type of structure, where the work of magic or religious rites is done, whereas its cousin, the shrine, is more of a box or reliquary kind of creature, usually for the veneration or worship of a specific being or deity. I have the shrines to several spirits that are kept near the altar where I do most of my work.

2   Our vessel meant here as the whole of ourselves and our work, mundane and magical, both sacred and profane.

speak to its maker of magic, and of power.

I add further bits, usually sigils, vessels of particular Spirits or for particular aims, and talismans. These serve to bring the Powers and Spirits I am working with into synchrony, into a unity of purpose. This is all artistic, aesthetic, and driven by gut-feel. My own space feels incomplete these days without my two Finnish knives and a terra-cotta skull from Mexico. If something seems off, move or remove it. The end result should itself be magical. As it grows in time (in a psychic sense, as in growing in power and clarity, becoming more "itself") fueled by the work done at it (spells, rituals, energy work), via the candles, incense or other offerings given, this sense should build.

My altar has a lot of natural items on it. Skulls and bones from animals that suit me and my work. They remind me that I am like them, an animal, and also like them, alive for only a short while. Coyotes for their dawn and dusk travels and song, a bobcat for its stealth and vision, a goat for its deep ties to witchcraft and magic. Feathers and bones from a variety of birds (spirit flight and the playful genius of crows and ravens). Stones from special places, or simply stones that are themselves special. Sometimes I know what each item is for when I find it. Sometimes I simply know to bring it to the altar and welcome it in and know that I will understand the "why" behind it at some later date.

If you are in a particular tradition of practice, this may suggest or require specific sets of power symbols, gods, spirits, and tools, and you will be best served to work with these as given.

My symbol set tends towards sigils, and my aesthetic tends towards organic materials, bones, sticks, stones. I work with these things as tools, and they are both powerful and comforting to me. For example, the skulls I use are consecrated to the spirits I work with, and also work as triggers to my deep mind. Some of what is triggered is conscious, in that I am aware that I am asking for a particular type of energetic or spirit connection. Some of what is triggered is less clear to my conscious mind but speaks directly to my deep mind.

I might pick a particular piece, be it skull or bone, or jar-vessel, and use it to help focus the specific work I am doing. I have a bobcat skull that is consecrated to traveling, that I either hold or place near me when I trance. It's a good friend.

The altar in my approach is both shrine to the spirits I work with and working space. It is the (inside the house) physical nexus of my sorcery. It serves as a focal point, fuel cell, and information center for the work. It is where I steer the ship from, where I go to ask for aid, where I go to feed the Spirits I work with. And so it reflects me and my work. So it needs to be for each person, a reflection of the individual and their work, their allies.

I have friends whose working altars are filled with flowers, deity statues, and are filled with bright colors. These suit their owners' working styles perfectly. I know people who have unmarked wooden blocks to represent the various powers. There is no standard approach nor is there a need for one outside of established traditions.

If you have never built a working altar before, here are some concepts to start with. What turns you on to do magic? What slips itself between your ribs to touch your heart? What sings a song of sorcery, of spirit, of possibility? This might be a vase of roses, a skull, a bullet, a stone, an image of a god, an angel, or an animal. A geometric form. It's all fair game as long as it speaks to you at the gut level of magic and power.

This can become a central image or icon. After the central piece, what are the other powers you work with? A tool, vessel, image of something that links to whatever you work with for protection. Your focus for prosperity and wealth work. Offering bowls or other vessels for the Spirits. Candle holders. Your most regularly used tools. For me, these are my Finnish knives, and my scribe I use for marking sigils and runes into candles.

Out and about I find altars all over. Between two trees, on a low wall at an abandoned house. There is a feel to these places. Follow the power, the gut, that knife-in-heart bright heat.

The altar is a space between the worlds. It is a bridge, a door, a gate that opens from this world into all others. There is no "necessary" structure for it, other than that it sings to you.

MATERIAL BASES

One of the easiest ways to improve the manifestation of tangible results in magic is to incorporate material bases. A material base is any solid object consecrated or made special to a task, intention, or spirit. By creating a link in the world of "hard goods" we can send a clear message to all parties concerned: make this real in this material world that my body inhabits.

Outside of trance work, meditation, breath work, and energy work, pretty much all other kinds of work will be more successful if linked to a material base.

Likewise, a sigil or magical seal will work better in the material world once made manifest in a physical form. It may be it drawn on paper or fashioned in wax, wood, or metal. That it is pretty doesn't matter as much as that you can touch it with your hands, breathe on it, and the like.

The creation of altars and material bases are the concretization of magical intentions. Follow the power in their construction, working from the gut. Include only those elements you are choosing to give power to in your life and practice. Periodically tend to and clean them, removing anything whose importance has faded, and re-iterate your current desires as you reset them. I do this on the new and full moon with good results.

CHAPTER TWENTY TWO

THE WORK OF THE WEAVERS

Sorcery reveals itself in time. Sometimes we do a piece of work and the results happen at that moment. This is true of trance work, where we might "go" somewhere and meet someone who will aid us or show us something. It is also the case when we evoke a spirit and it teaches us something right then. Perhaps we make a sigil to find our keys, and we find our keys a few moments later. This is not actually the norm.

More often, we do the work, and some time later we realize that what we worked for has come to pass. Sometimes we halfway-almost-decide to do the work, and then realize that the "result" is already coming when we haven't actually done the work yet![1]

I liken magic to a wooden ship for this reason. To build a ship, there is a design to be made, a plan for turning trees into a seaworthy vessel. There are trees to fell, then to cut and carve into planks. There are sails to be sewn out of cloth that needs to be woven, and masts and oars and rudders to make and fit. Gaps to be discovered and filled to keep the sea out. Then a crew to assemble, stores to be collected and stowed. At last, a good day to launch. So it is with magic.

Some of the Northern Europeans believed in a form of the Fates called the Norns, also known as the Wyrd Sisters.[2] They were called Urda, Verdandi, and Skuld. Their names mean What Was, What Is, and What Shall Be. In this story (and most of the ways we describe how things work are just stories, even if we choose to believe them) the Wyrd Sisters literally weave your life, your Wyrd, from birth to death and beyond. Once, conditions arose from causes that led to your conception and birth. In other words, your parent's parents met, in a particular time, in a particular place, and so your parents were born. Likewise with your parents meeting, leading to your own birth. These are the close-in causes and

---

1 A word to the wise: do the work anyway! Really, just do it.

2 And some of us still do!

conditions from which you have risen up, the causal chain that has led to your being alive now to read this book. We each have what is a bit like our root-destiny, our root causes and conditions. This is inherited in part, and partly acquired by our actions. This is Urda's realm, and is all that has happened up until this very moment. The now is Verdandi's realm and is always becoming, and always being handed back to Urda as it passes. Who you were, based on causes and conditions now past, who you are now and what you do this very instant will lead you irrevocably into Skuld's realm, that which is to come.

The idea that our personal Wyrd, our destiny, is a work in progress, not an outright predetermined Fate, allows us agency, the option to choose different roads and doors. This is the Weaving of Wyrd.

There are some peculiarities, however. We cannot (or at least I cannot) change the actual events of the past. But we can to a large degree change what effects they have on us now. This is sometimes clearer than other times. Have you ever had a bad thing happen that years later you realized that while still "bad," maybe even horrible, had completely positive outcomes? This begins to touch on the edges of what I am speaking of.

If you look at the text of the Re/Claiming rite, you'll see that I have you repeatedly end the statements with some version of "As it was, as it is, and as it shall be."[3] This is a request that the work we do affects us on all levels: past, present, and future. The psychological take on this is that perhaps this allows us to re-write our experience of the past and its effects on the present. I would only add to that: "and maybe not just on the psychological but on the psychic level as well."

By consciously choosing to state that we can touch all three strands of time, we can exist in a better version of the present, while mitigating some of the least helpful aspects of the past and weaving a better future.

Can you do sigils or other kinds of sorcery to change the current effects of past events? That is an interesting question, and one worth exploring.

---

3   Stolen from the Church, along with the gold candlesticks. What works, works!

CHAPTER TWENTY THREE

PLAYING THE LONG GAME

Why are you where you are right now? In your life, job, relationships, health? Take these questions into your practices. What do you find when you ask about them in meditation? What does the pendulum say? The tarot? Your astrologer? Your psychologist or counselor? Can you see the path that led to where you are now from where you were in the past? If you can, these two points form a line of sorts, which can be projected forward in time, to where you are going. This is rarely anything like a straight line, but more of a general bearing, an overall direction. Where we come from is a controlling factor that overall we can't change. This can suck, like if we really wanted to be a pro basketball player but have shit genetics for that sport. But what we actually decide to do with what we are given is of crucial importance. Django Reinhardt and Tony Iommi both became hugely influential guitar players with badly injured hands that would have stopped most people from even bothering to try. They did this in the now. They looked at the hands they were dealt (no pun intended), what the past influences were, and adjusted their courses to get them where they truly wanted to go. They made conscious decisions to persevere and learn new methods that allowed them to succeed. This is all we can ever do.

We can bring magic to bear on this in many ways. The first requires honestly assessing our situation. Meditation, divination, mapping on paper all can help here. What past events are your main controllers? In my case, for whatever reason, for the first twenty years or more of my life, I didn't think I could do much of anything very well at all. This was a major controlling factor. It was the classic self-fulfilling prophecy. I "knew" I wasn't going to be very good at anything, so I never tried very hard. In time I began to see that this was not actually true, that I was rather good at a few things. What they were is not important, their existence was a crack in the wall called "not good enough." Starting with that first bit of light through the crack, I began using ritual to change this perception of "not very good at much of anything." I began to enchant for being good at things I desired. Sigils for "I do anything I set my mind to very well." Playing music, talking to people, meeting girls. And my clumsy methods worked very well.

How this actually worked was I realized I had a weak point or weak points that were rooted in family and grade school dynamics (I didn't really do high school). I didn't always know precisely the origin of these weak points, but I could place them in time fairly well.[1]

I looked at what I did *now* that reinforced these things. Wanting to be good at guitar rather than actually practicing. Spending time wishing I was comfortable talking to people instead of actually talking to them. Wishing I knew what to say to girls I was interested in rather than just talking to them (helpful hint: most people like to talk more than listen, so just ask questions in a friendly open manner and you will do fine socially, be this in meeting people in general, finding lovers, or getting along in the workplace. We only really have problems when we want to talk *and* be listened to in return. The people who will actually do this and enjoy it with us we call "friends").

So first there are the basic "mundane world" things, i.e., playing guitar every day even though you suck, asking strangers questions even though you are brutally uncomfortable. We can enchant for success in these endeavors as well.

Create a sigil or phrase (mantra) for what you are working on. I used "I play guitar to amuse myself" if I recall correctly. I ritualized the practice. I would light a candle and a stick of incense, and just play, trying to play whatever I was playing a bit better until the incense burned out. I would

---

1   It's good to watch tendencies to nail this kind of thing down to specific moment. While in some instances this can be helpful, in others it may be an oversimplification. We can fixate on a moment, perhaps one of violence, and in a sense use this to mask a larger reality. For example, a person could decide to lock down a fear of violence as being caused by getting beat up at a particular moment in time, which while perhaps quite traumatic may mask a more important truth, which is that they spent years living in a scenario where violence was always possible, even though it only actually manifested physically for them at that one moment. In such a scenario the chronic stressor (long term exposure to threats of violence) is actually more likely to be the "root" of their difficulties more than the single, acute event. This happens at a culture wide level for many people.

thank the guitar for hanging out with me. I would praise myself for any slight improvement, or even just for practicing if I couldn't see any.

I once did a sigil for talking to strangers and made up a verbal spell along the lines of "what do I find interesting about you?" to notice things I liked about the people I ran across.[2] This might be their shoes, hair, what they were reading, their bicycle. I would remember the sigil and the spell when I would get uncomfortable, and this gave me the mental space to actually open my mouth and say something. I said a lot of stupid shit. This was fine, as it was all part of the ritual!

This is not all psychological, though our psychology is a huge piece of it. It is using our psychology in conjunction with our sorcery to bring about a change of state. It is realizing that past events, lessons learned, and primarily, damages endured have all worked to set us on a track, like a train. If we do not choose to become aware of the tracks and decide to leave them, however difficult or uncomfortable that is, we *will* go where they lead. Which is usually pretty much where we are now, carried out forever.

So we use the past to see what we are doing now and how much this reflects the life we desire. The main controller of where you are going is what you do now. Make friends with Verdandi.

To put this into practice, write out a letter, something along these lines. You can use this text to start if you like. Remember: pen on paper, as this requires a material base.

"Here and now, ever and always I choose my path. I am the arbiter of my destiny. I am born of what was, I am built from what came before, but I am not ruled by it. I am the one who decides. I am the one who rules in the present. I am the one who chooses the weight and measure of my past. I am the one whose direction lies *forward*. I am the one who gains the skills I need to be and do what I choose to be and do. I am the one to decides what is important to me. I claim my birthright as magician. I claim my birthright as an avatar of the ineffable. I choose the road I walk, and I walk it in full knowledge that I have chosen it. I walk it knowing that I alone can

---

2   This is indeed magic. It is an increase in communication with the Field and its inhabitants, it is a ritual action to bring about change, and was highly effective. Sorcery is not all about candles and demons!

walk it and that I alone can choose another path. I take full and complete responsibility for my actions from this moment forward. Here and now, ever and always, I choose my path."

Take this letter to your altar, or out into nature. Read it aloud daily until you feel its truth in your bones. Let it kindle a fire inside you. Let it burn away all of the voices that deny its truth.

Now continue this process. What hinders you? Cast it aside. Bring it to the altar, write it out, say goodbye to it and burn the paper. Watch it burn, and know that as fire transforms the paper and ink into ash and smoke, so it is with that which blocks you, that which hinders you.

What skills do you need to become who you desire? Write them down. Take them to the altar, call them to you. Do the mundane work to gain them, as enchantment without concrete mundane world action to aid its manifestation is so unlikely to lead to success as to not be worth considering as an approach.

Build an engine of your desires, your Wills.[3] Feed it constantly. Enchant on all levels for them. Weed out false desires, those which are not really that important. Decide if those desires "imported" from others or from your culture are truly relevant. Keep them if they are, and take them to the altar and lay claim to them in the here and now. If they are not relevant, take them to the altar as well and let them go. Ritualize the letting go. If they persist (our parents' dreams for us are often tenacious, and may have nothing to do with our own, for example), clear them out. Take them into meditation, ritually divest yourself from them. Own what is yours, and walk away from what is not. Boost the signal of what you are, what you will be, and turn down the volume on all of the extraneous noise.

---

3   "Wills" in a magical sense, rather than a singular "true will." What we are working towards manifesting, our intentions. Thus plural, as most of us "will" be working on any number of intentions at a given time!

A BRIEF NOTE ON TIME

While I don't pay too much attention to astrology, I do pay a lot of attention to the moon. I find no reasonable way at all to ignore the lunar cycle from a magical perspective. This is pretty straightforward and doesn't change much for most people.

The lunar cycle is defined by quarters.

> New Moon – dark to half (waxing)
> First Quarter – half to full
> Full Moon – full to half (waning)
> Third Quarter – half waning to dark

In general, as the moon is waxing (growing bigger), light is increasing and so is the available "current" for magical work. As it becomes full and sits at full brightness, this current is at its strongest. As it wanes and grows ever slimmer and less bright, the current also fades. The current is at its lowest point when the moon is dark.

The standard approach is to, when possible, do work for increase as the moon is waxing, as it increases in brightness and fullness. This is the preferred time for drawing things to yourself, increasing income and the like. After the full moon, as the moon is decreasing, this is a good time to do work for decrease and elimination, sending things away, casting off old habits, and taking out the trash.

For me, well, I kind of go to shit energetically around the three days of the dark moon. It's nothing horrible, but I don't plan to be particularly useful to anyone on those days.

After the dark days, I get a major boost of energy, focus, and clarity as the crescent moon reappears. This actually runs to the full moon until a few days before the dark. So the short form is, I have two weeks out of the month, from the first sliver of the waxing crescent to the full moon that are better suited for most of the work that I do magically, as the majority is for increase.

During this period, I might do work for improving my business, building new relationships, doing healing work, renewing protective work, etc. This is all increase or "drawing" work, as in drawing something to me. If I am consecrating talismans or creating/starting new vessels, I tend to do that work during the waxing moon as well.[4]

For the work of decrease, the time beginning several days after the full moon until the dark is preferred. This is also the traditional time to lay curses, for those so inclined. I am not much for cursing (or hitting people, which is pretty much the same thing but in the mundane world), but it is an excellent time to purge. Clean your altars, discard anything you have attracted that no longer serves, and generally clean house.

4   This is far, far from a hard and fast rule. Any type of work can be done at any time, although doing work for increase with a truly no-light dark moon will likely need to be repeated or added to once the waxing crescent shows, in my experience.

CHAPTER TWENTY FOUR

SACRED FEAR

There is a type of fear that is holy.

Holy terror or sacred fear comes to some (everyone who will open to it, I believe) at moments in the practice of sorcery. Sometimes it is a warning: "Really? You really want to go *here*?" Sometimes it is a meeting with a power that is so, so present, and so much Other that the senses rebel and recoil at the presence. The main thing to understand is that this kind of fear is information. It is related to the fear when the rattlesnake rattles nearby, or you see a mountain lion on a ledge not very far from you, watching.

This kind of fear is a natural response to particular kinds of power. It is not necessarily a response to an actual threat.

I remember a time in the high mountains near Mt. Shasta where I came upon a snow-melt lake, right at the tree line. I slept near the lake and awoke to this kind of terror. I lay in my sleeping bag inside my tent, holding tight to an earlier incarnation of the Finnish knife, shaking. I could "hear" the breath of a big animal right outside the tent. In time it settled into a purr, and what seemed like hours later I realized it had moved off. I made myself get up, get dressed and leave the tent while it was still dark. The world was electric with power, the stars biting clear, up there around ten thousand feet. After a while, still terror-ridden, I walked to the edge of the snow-melt lake. The stars were reflected in the water, but there were other lights there, moving. These were flashes like lightning, bolt-blue, rising from the lake bottom to the surface, hundreds of them, over and over. The terror shifted to awe, and then to fascination. I sat and watched the witch-lights in the water until dawn, when they faded. In the growing light, I saw movement on the other side of the lake. The mountain lion who had awoken me to see this sight, moving down the mountain in the morning light.

Another time, when I was eleven, I dreamed I was in a bookstore, a place in Berkeley, California called, appropriately enough, Dark Carnival. This was my preferred source for books back then. I felt a brutal cold wind all of a sudden, and I looked up. There before me was a vision of the Man in Black, though I had no idea who the hell that was back then! He stood before me, black suit, black beard, black hair, black eyes, and pretty much blasted me into oblivion with his power. The effect was one of total terror and pure awe. He carried with him a field of force so intense that the only response I could have had to it was fear. It was all-encompassing, leaving nothing but its own echo when I awoke.

After both of these experiences, my life completely changed.

You may encounter this kind of fear out and about in the world, or at your altar, or in your bed. In most cases, it is information. Listen (perceive) to the best of your ability to what that information is telling you. It may be a transmission of power, and it may be a warning. Some people should not enter some places. Just as there are healing, helpful places of power, so are there hurtful ones.

Sometimes the fear is telling you "get ready, get into your power, this is a rough space and you need to be AWAKE" and sometimes it is telling you that you don't belong, and you best get your ass home while it is all in one piece. No one else can interpret these things for you.

One other bit of fear related thought. If you practice magic, over time you begin to be recognized by the Others. The work will make you more interesting to them, and not just the helpful, friendly ones. Not all of this attention will be welcome. Do the work suggested in the "Stay Clean" chapter, and understand that while the individual instance may not be pleasant and may produce effects that need to be handled, this is a side effect that comes of actually doing the work. It is not a "bad" thing any more than a virus or a broken bone, or getting too close to a strange dog's home is a "bad" thing. These are natural events, even if unpleasant or scary.

I can't tell you what to do with any these kinds of fear, only that they are not uncommon. Remember that they are information-dense reactions to power and will need to be addressed according to each particular person and situation.

CHAPTER TWENTY FIVE

ON CONSECRATION, A CANDLE SPELL AND FALLING IN LOVE

To consecrate something is to make it special. We can do this in a variety of ways, either separately or combined together.

For example, let's say I am burning a candle to enfold someone in protection. I have a scribe (like a big iron needle for marking lines on metal) that I use to carve sigils or runes into the wax of the candle. Perhaps I am using the Algiz rune for this. Algiz is a good protection rune, and looks like this:

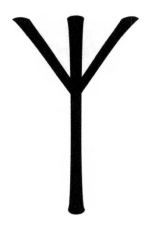

THE RUNE ALGIZ

How I do this is pretty straightforward. I inscribe the rune into the wax with the needle. I lick or spit on the rune to moisten it and link it to me (only done for work I want directly linked or connected to me). I may anoint it with an oil to bring another influence to the work. I may add powdered herbs or dusts of some sort, and I may redden the rune with red sandalwood powder.[1] I then put the candle in the holder and speak whatever "spell" I am using, which for me is usually plainspoken. Rhymes and poetry are great, but I find that I am more clear and honest if I just speak (or I may just be a poor poet!). Let us pretend that I am doing this work for a person named Julia.

Here's how this might actually work in practice:

> I have gathered a candle, a protection powder,[2] red sandalwood powder, a lighter, an oil, and my needle-scribe.
>
> I pick up the candle and say out loud: *"Creature of wax and wick, I ask that you work with me to aid and guard Julia."*
>
> I take up the scribe and say: *"Creature of iron, I ask that you work with me to aid and guard Julia."*
>
> I etch the rune into the wax, saying: *"Beautiful Algiz, bright and sharp, I ask that you work with me to aid and guard Julia."*
>
> I lick or spit on the rune and say: *"By the water of my life do I give life to you that you may aid and guard Julia."* (Omit this step for any working you do not want linked directly to you!)[3]
>
> I place a drop of oil on the rune and rub it in saying: *"Creature of oil, bless this creature of wax, and join with it to aid and guard Julia."*

1   I tend to the red sandalwood, but also use other natural pigment colors – powdered pigments likes ochres, siennas, and umbers work well to "redden" the candles. Red ochre has a very long history of use for reddening bones.

2   A word on powders and dusts. You can buy these, but the best are homemade. They are basically any *materia* appropriate to the work you are doing, ground as close to powder as possible. With a mortar and pestle the work can be considerable to make them, but that is all time and energy well spent on focusing the intention. A coffee grinder is certainly quicker! If you follow the general instructions for consecration you end up with a very potent, focus-specific power booster.

3   This was pointed out by a reader as odd, the licking of the candle for work not for myself. In most cases, I would not suggest this. However, in the scenario I imagined when writing this chapter, "Julia" was someone very close to me. I therefore used my saliva to intentionally create a link to me. In a sense, I am placing myself into the situation directly. "You want to mess with my friend? Then you are messing with me, and all that comes with me!" So it is a way of further enfolding Julia in protection by standing with her directly. This is not something I would do for anyone I was not *very* close to!

I sprinkle the protection herbs on the rune and rub them in saying: *"Creature of the fertile Earth, join with your brethren to aid and guard Julia."*

I add the red sandalwood powder and say *"I redden this rune, I consecrate this creature of wax with spit, with oil, with herbs, with iron, and with the breath of my body (breathe upon the rune). Creature of wax, I give you life that you may aid and guard Julia."*

Mount the candle in a holder, and light it, saying: *"Creature of fire, kindle the flame, awaken this creature of power to aid and guard Julia."*

Simple and direct is usually the most effective method.

ANOTHER APPROACH

Falling in love. That's a thing, isn't it? Sorcery, if I may say so, is so much like falling in love as to sometimes be the same thing.

Imagine taking a piece of wood. And a small pocket knife. And sitting by a fire, or somewhere in the sun. And thinking about something that you would really like to have happen. Sharpen the knife as you think about it. How it could come to pass, all the different ways. As you sharpen the blade, think of all the possible ways and as many impossible ways, unknown ways, unimaginable ways it could come to pass as you can. When the knife is good and sharp, turn your attention to the wood. Ask it if it would like to help you with your desire. It probably would like to! I've never had a piece of wood say "no!" Tell it what you desire (unless it actually is being difficult and really does say "no way!" in which case just try a different piece of wood. There's no need to be rude). Ask it if it has a form inside of itself that it would like to take. Perhaps a circle? A bear? A fish? A moon? If it seems like it would like to be a particular form, go with that and begin carving away the excess. It doesn't need to be high art, you are just seeking a sense, an essence. If you don't get a hit on a particular shape, anything will work. A simple sphere, egg, cylinder, simply pick something that seems good to you. Now talk to the piece of wood. Tell it of your desire. Tell it of the various ways you have thought of that you could see your desire coming to pass. Be sure to let your new friend know that you are open to other ways, that you know you cannot see everything possible from your vantage point. Ask your wood-friend to find a good way to bring your desire about, if it could be so kind. As you carve the piece, see if it tells you something. This may be explicit, as in a voice or a vision (be careful with the knife!) or more subtle, just a sense that all will be well, or that perhaps something else may be needed. Pay attention, listen (by which I mean "be open to sense impressions of all sorts"), and work with the knife until the piece seems done. Now spit on your hands, and rub it into the wood. Breathe onto (into) your ally to give it life. Perhaps pass it through smoke to give it warmth if it is present. Does a particular oil or perfume come to mind? Give it that. All the while, keep conversing with it while leaving quiet spaces to listen. When you both feel "done," you can either carry the object with you, place it in a special place where you can see it frequently, or perhaps hide it away to spend time with in secret.

This is magic, and if done with intention, and devotion, it should feel a bit like falling in love.

The above is only one way. The same can be done with fabric, yarn, clay, metal. It can be a painting, a story, a book (this book?).

Magic is the art of falling in love with the Field and its inhabitants.

CHAPTER TWENTY SIX

VESSELS

A container is an item in which objects, materials or data can be stored or transported, says the dictionary. A vessel specifically carries fluid, like a bottle or jar or even a blood vessel, but can also be a boat or ship, something that can carry us as well. In this combined sense, a blend of all the above, we will approach this work.

As we ourselves carry within us a multitude of cells, bodily structures, and organs, we also carry ideas, memories, dreams, talents, skills, as well as the body and spirit memories of those people who come before us, blood relatives or not. I am as much a child of the spirits as I am of my parents and have as-deep-as-blood ties to several spirit-lines. We are vessels.

Vessels can hold disparate elements together, and can also function like a magical boiler. As boilers, vessels can help to build magical "pressures," to contain them and give them focus and direction, like a sorcerous steam engine.

Looking to hoodoo for an example, we can look at the honey or sugar jar as a basic format. In this case, we would make a petition for something we want to draw to us. We place the completed petition into the jar, along with other things that seem relevant. We fill the jar with sugar (I am a meddler, and it's much cleaner to work with sugar than with honey!), leaving some room at the top so you can literally "shake it up" to put some motion into the jar, to get things moving when they slow down or stagnate.

Mason type jars with metal lids are commonly used for this kind of work as you can burn candles on the metal tops without starting a fire. But this type of thing can be done in bottles, or metal cans with tight lids, like some kinds of tea tins.

A bag spell is a similar idea. You place a collection of objects that relate to the work at hand into a smallish bag, perhaps of a particular color or pattern, consecrating everything as usual, and tie or sew it shut. It can then be carried in a pocket, stitched into clothing, or tucked in a pillow, which is a favorite method for dream work.

Boxes are often used as containers for magic. A drawing box might be created that incorporates a master sigil into its design, say for a business, for learning a skill, for increasing anything in your life. The box itself is consecrated, embellished, sigilized. As the project proceeds, further helpful elements are added to the box, be they sigils, petitions, stones, herbs, curios, or images.

I tend to combine techniques, using many approaches to achieve my aims. So I might have a sugar jar for my business that has a master sigil built into it for overall success, which I place more specific pieces (the smaller goals or helpers) into in petition or sigil form. It becomes a house for the overall work of building and keeping my business happy and healthy. If I realize I need more work in one area, I can add the appropriate sigil to the existing shoal that dwells inside the vessel. I can feed the vessel by burning candles on it, shake it up (adding motion, waking it up) or heat it or cool it as needed.[1]

A last method is to make a vessel yourself, out of clay. I've dug my own clay for this at times, but store-bought clay works fine. Using whatever potting skills you have (or don't have, if you are like me!), build yourself a clay jar. Sigilize it as you work, and form your intentions into the material continuously. It helps (I learned this the hard way) to have your cork or stopper ready when you are forming your vessel this way! Once it is fully formed, fire your vessel to harden it and bring it to life.

If you have done this with full intentionality and consecrated your vessel as you made it, it should come out of the fire a bit lively. Finish it with whatever paints, stains, and sigils are appropriate to the work. Now there are a few ways to proceed. When I have made these vessels, I placed them in a wooden box to protect them, and buried them for a time. This might be a specific number of days or months that are appropriate to the work, or for a lunar cycle. You might make your vessel near the full moon and dig it up again at the next full moon, or several cycles later. When you unearth it, the vessel is to be viewed as being born. It should be welcomed into the world of the living, and it should be "fed" with offerings suited to its nature. I usually choose to not place anything that would rot inside the

---

1   The heating and cooling in this case may only be metaphorical, but it is not always so. There are times when actually heating things on a stove or over a candle, or placing them in the freezer may make sense.

vessel, so give it dry *materia* as "food." Once it has been unearthed and fed, it can be brought into the home or working space and introduced to the family, so to speak.

This process is a form of servitor creation (or spirit-calling depending on your point of view), and should be approached with forethought as it is intended to be in some senses "alive," and will have more of an active sentience than most servitors. It is not a good idea to make these and then forget about them!

CHAPTER TWENTY SEVEN

TALISMANIC MAGIC

I think of a talisman as the root-level type of material base for the work of magic. It can be a vessel, a creature, a storehouse, a key, a gate. It can be made or found, crafted or bought. A talisman is always personal, in use if not in construction.

The talisman is a meeting point of power, will, desire, intention, and action. An altar can be a talisman, as can be the cup, knife, pantacle,[1] and the skull that sits upon it.

A sorcerer seeks power.[2] Not necessarily in the larger, social sense, but in the sense of seeking powerful currents that lead to where they are going, much like a ship's captain who seeks to place her vessel into the current that will carry her home. These currents of power share a common tone to me, which is a sense of inevitability. Have you had the experience of reading a book, and far before you have enough information to know where it is going, you can feel the pull towards an inevitable, inexorable conclusion? That feeling or pull is similar to my sense of currents of magical power.

A sorcerer seeks power. This is a somewhat oracular experience. You see something, perhaps a card, a note, a feather, and it sort of hums or sings. It has a pull, a gravity, a sense of agency. It offers choices: pick me up, or don't. Listen to me, or don't. Step into this current, or don't.

A sorcerer seeks power. One of the possible etymologies of sorcery I

---

1   A pantacle is a magical tool, usually a painted or inscribed disk.

2   This meaning of power, as Starhawk so well put it in her book *Truth or Dare,* is power-from-within and also power-with-others rather than the more coercion and domination based power-over-others. These are the natural currents of magical energy and potency, as well as spirits and such that we may choose to work with. There are moments when one may find they have to exert power-over in magic, but I personally find this is better avoided. Put another way, it's better (or at least easier!) to be discerning about who you let into the house than kicking out those who get wasted and start breaking things!

found years ago is "one who lays out lots." This was intended I expect as a reference to divination, of casting lots, runes, cards, bones to see what is, what was, and how things will come to pass given the current course of actions and events, causes and conditions. But a "lot" is also a fate, a destiny. To lay out destinies or fates is to choose a direction, what it looks like, feels like, tastes like and to manifest it. To decide, given how the present state has arisen, and what form it has taken, what can be done now to move in the direction of the "what is to come" that best suits the operant.

If she can find that current of power, that pull of a possible future, and steer her ship into it, our enchantress can more easily arrive at that place.

This is all multi-sensory, a merging of inner and outer senses that shows us where the flowing of power is naturally moving to. We don't as much steer the actual magical current as steer *into* it, and then ride it. The more clearly we can see and feel what we are, the more likely we are to be able to see what we need.

Delusion is the main hindrance here. Delusion means we don't know who we really are, or how we actually came to be where we are now, and so we cannot perceive our situation or self accurately enough to find our way forward. We may find ourselves stuck in a current moving us away from where we seek to go. Trapped in an eddy, spinning. Waiting for it to turn into a maelstrom before we try to fight our way out. Delusion allows this all to happen. It obscures causes and conditions, and it happens when we lie to ourselves or misunderstand the information we receive for whatever reason. The psychic censor is a master of delusion.

The generation or use of talismanic objects that are "clearly what they are"[3] can help us in this process. They can serve as reminders. You are protected. You have an ally. You have a line on a current of power. They can help us to avoid distraction and delusion. They can tell us: "You are powerful, so don't be a dork and operate like someone who isn't. You have tools so you don't have to try to muddle through without them, use them!"

The talisman is a vessel, which can hold power. I often meditate or trance with talismans in hand. This both aids in the trance, and allows me

---

3   "What they are": touchstones and power objects with a strong embedded or indwelling nature towards a particular means or end. Said another way a talisman is a cause and condition leading to a specific (or specific type of) outcome, state, action or spirit contact.

to "place" or connect the talisman to the desired state when it comes to pass. This placement is of a moment: I note the current, and I "set it" into the talisman, a bit like touching a button to store a contact in a phone. I often trance with a key or road opener type of talisman in one hand, and that of an ally or desired target or contact in the other.

Here is a way to build a talisman that I have been playing with a lot in the past year.

Get some tough cord, I use the Chinese nylon bead stringing cord, as it's incredibly strong, and a selection of beads that speak to your intentions. I avoid plastic, but use stone, metal, wood, bone. You can add a charm or symbol if you like, but it is not needed.

Arrange the beads in an order, one bead for each word of a prayer, phrase, or mantra that directly feeds into the work you are doing and what you are building this talisman-creature for.

Write out a petition, and then re-assemble the letters into a new "sentence" of nonsense words that sound good and strong to you. This part is like building a verbal sigil, with less intention towards simplification, and more towards tone and vibration of sounds.

Let's pick an intention of: "A power source for trance work." We rearrange the letters, forming new words in an unknown (to our conscious mind) language. We follow the power and the flow of sounds. Maybe we end up with: ROAS FOREN KOUR PRETO CEWAK.

We have a five "word" mantra now, and in this example, we have decided to make a talismanic mala of nine sets of five beads. I like to use "odd" beads for the beginning and end of each pass of our "mantra." Maybe just larger or rougher textured beads, or sometimes I will knot the cord between each set instead, leaving a gap. This allows me to trance out, but know where I am in the mantra if I lose track.

Now we have a collection of beads that match the words of our intention.[4] We set about cultivating them into a talisman via consecration as we build it. With each bead I add, each knot I tie, I speak my intention, I

---

4 I hope it is obvious that this can be used in a less sigilized way, you can use any string of words of power that suit you. This is happening in most Eastern-influenced mala work, and using the IAO SABAOTH portion of the Headless Rite worked well for me.

ask its assistance, I thank it. Once it is made, and fully consecrated, I use it towards its purpose. I chant out the mantra and count the beads as part of the trance induction. If I start to "slip" out of trance, I might use the chant to bring myself back in. As I use the bead-string over time, it becomes more the creature it is (as "you are what you do" is true for animals like humans, so it is for magical beings like talismans).[5] As I imprint the current into it by using it, so it becomes a "key" or guide to finding that current in the future. This is one way to approach the laying-out of fate. We build the tools and cultivate the allies we need to create the life we want and which will assist us to stay on course to its manifestation.

You can use these techniques with your found objects as well. You can ask them for their words of power. Sit with them, and perhaps start vocalizing the vowels. Find the tones that speak to the talisman, or that let it speak to you. Ask for its aid. Ask it what it likes (and feel free to get it onto another track if it gets crazy. Because it says it likes blood and solid gold by the pound doesn't mean it actually needs them or that you should give them to it!). Become friends, see if you can work together, or if your ways of being clash too much for that. If you do clash, be polite. Thank it, give it a small offering, and move on.

The talisman as I view it is a vessel-creature-power-being, and it can take most possible forms. A book can be a talisman, as can a bird's foot or feather. A piece of music can be. The sorcerer can generate a brief passage to play musically while working, keeping the intention in mind, perhaps focusing on its sigil. She can get into the current she seeks to work with via any method, and use the voice, guitar, piano, flute or drum to move deeper and more fully into the current. Now she has a talisman of sound. People who knit, knit power into their work, as wood carvers cut and carve it in, and boat builders, bakers, painters, singers all can do the same within their respective arts. This does not mean that every act is talismanic, but that every art can be used to produce a talisman. Lovers might bind each other via the creatures they build with their sweat, saliva, and sexual fluids. You can try and tell me how this isn't happening unintentionally anyway and I'll laugh at you. Actual children are the obvious result, but subtler versions are ever-present.

---

5   It is worth looking into and thinking on the SAID (Specific Adaptation to Imposed Demands) principle as it relates to this.

Talismans can also be less conscious. We can accept enchantment at face value. We find the bone, the ring, the stone, and it speaks to us. I once found a "lucky" pistol cartridge. Why that one was lucky when so many of them are not, I will never know. We do not need to have a clear understanding of the exact words to describe the talisman. We see it, touch it, and ask ourselves "does this connect to a current I seek?"

We do need to be wise, as sometimes this method can lead us a bit astray. Something decidedly too enchanting might be on its own mission, so to speak. Such a find may require a bit of investigation to determine if its intentions are legit and congruent with our own. Ulterior motives abound in sorcery as much as in any other kind of relationship!

We can ask the same of the herbs and other *materia* we use in magic, being intelligent about what we actually do in light of their suggestions. The Datura-laced brownies are probably not a good idea (at all!), although the Datura spirits might suggest otherwise! While we need not be overly reliant on correspondences gained elsewhere, they can definitely be of use at times. Know your poisons, and you won't stray too far.

The end point is common sense: the proof is always, always, always in the pudding. If something screams out to you "I'll bring you luck!" and your whole life collapses when it is around...well, perhaps it wasn't being entirely honest, or it meant the other kind of luck. Your work should move you closer to your goals, closer to the current that moves you forward. If it does otherwise, a change of course is in order. Magic is taking responsibility for all aspects of your life, and the ability to make a decision to change it is the most basic freedom of all.

CHAPTER TWENTY EIGHT

BEHIND THE WALL OF SLEEP

I met the Man in Black in a dream when I was eleven years old.

When I was eighteen, in a fever brought on by a magical attack from a lake I had offended, I dreamt of a battle for three days, died over and over, and learned how to win that battle.

When I met St. Cyprian it was in a dream, and he and a King performed bloody sorcerous surgery on me with huge old kitchen knives in an underground tomb.

The Dreaming, to use Neil Gaiman's term, is where we experience a large part of our life. Behind the wall of sleep lies another world, another universe. It is inexorably linked to the wake-world. We experience it, as we experience all things, through the medium of our body.

This body of ours is a material base. This is relevant and bears repeating. If we are indeed magical beings (as all beings that I have met are), then it makes sense to me that the general logic that prevails in our working with the Others is the same logic that prevails when working with our selves.[1] This is perhaps more obvious in the Dreaming than in many other places in our lives.

The foundational practice for dream work is to write down your dreams. William S. Burroughs kept index cards by the bed for this,[2] I use a book and a small digital recorder. If your dream recall is not as good as you would like it to be, write down everything you do remember, and I do mean everything.

A good way to start is to write every night before bed "I remember my dreams." Every morning, record anything you can. "Can't remember last night's dream, but I know I dreamt" is totally fine. But work to get something, anything. "I dreamt that it was cold" is totally useful, as you are training your mind to view what occurs in the Dreaming as important,

---

1 Selves, multiple. Where is this clearer than in the Dreaming?
2 William S. Burroughs, *My Education, A Book of Dreams*.

and not to be discarded.

Record your dreams when you wake at the first possible moment. I use a digital recorder I can operate without opening my eyes, and just babble it out. Later I record it into a dream journal. Your dream journal, be it a book or index cards, is a material base. Physically write down your dreams by hand, somewhere.

In time your dream recall will improve, and this allows more options. You can write down "I wish to re-visit the city by the sea" that you previously dreamt of. These things all become viable in time.

I am not a big one for interpretation of dreams, either by dream dictionary or dream analysis. I choose to view the dreaming as another life, and I would no more analyze the hidden meaning of the cat I met in a dream than I would the cat that is sitting on my foot. Many people receive great value from analysis, it is just not for me at this time.

We can, of course, apply magic to the process. I first learned a version of this working from Andrew Chumbley's book *Azoetia*.[3] Create a small bed that can reside beneath the bed you sleep on. If you have a bed on a frame with space beneath, this can be something like a doll's bed or a box with a "mattress" and linens. I've used the box from wooden matches for this with good results. If your mattress is on the floor, or some kind of solid frame, make the bed of paper or cloth. I've made nice ones out of bandanas before. Make it so you can tuck something under the "covers." If it ends up a more 3D doll's bed kind of thing, you could fashion a poppet (doll) of your dreaming self to place inside. For myself, I usually place a small "link" to myself, perhaps a packet of hair, an old piece of jewelry, or a photo.

Consecrate every piece as has been suggested before: *"This that I build is my dreaming bed, an aid to slip into that world, to move freely with no obstructions, and to be protected there from all harm"* and so on. Bring in whatever protective elements you require, perhaps an angelic link if you work with the Archangels or a link to whatever guardian spirit you personally work with. Build those items into the framework of the dreaming bed.

Once the dreaming bed is fully built and consecrated, place the dreaming bed beneath your bed. Keep it to your side of the bed if sleeping with others, although you may still get some bleed through! This can be

3   Andrew D. Chumbley, *Azoetia*, Xoanon.

mitigated by not actually sleeping on top of it, but by keeping it on an altar or secret place and taking a link to it to bed with you.

Create a dream petition or sigil to aid your dream-work. If you are not getting the kind of recall you desire, that would be a good focus. You could focus on one of the directions of the Six Ways, to learn more about that place. You could ask to meet a particular kind of ally in the dreaming.

Once the petition or sigil has been built and consecrated and charged it gets tucked into the dream-bed. I like to make a link to the dream-bed. In my case, I use my Gate of Dreams sigil drawn onto the top of the "bed-spread" of the dream bed and then wear the actual talisman to bed.

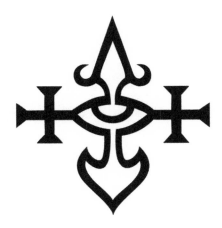

GATE OF DREAMS

In general, I find it helpful to not expect any particular result to come in any particular way. If we narrow the path by which a result must travel, we reduce the number of ways a desire can manifest. Enchant towards ends as much as possible, rather than means. This is as true in dream-work as it is in other areas.

Things that can help dream-work tend to be things that help sleep. Try to sleep in a very dark, preferably pitch-black room. Sleeping in a cooler room can help. If it's viable, try sleeping with earplugs. In the past, I have used herbal sleep teas of various sorts: passion flower, valerian root, skull-cap, catnip. A light tea of skullcap and catnip has been my main sleep aid for the past year.

Mugwort sachets under the pillow can often help with increasing dream activity, as can mugwort essential oils, or a sachet of Datura flowers tucked into a pillow. I have had great success using the relaxation parts of the trance induction as a sleep induction, as well.

Dream magic is like most other forms of magic: driven by attention, fed by communication, and responsive in the extreme to those who will interface with it in full integrity. Treat your dreams and the Dreaming appropriately, and they will so treat you in return.

CHAPTER TWENTY NINE

THE PROCESS OF WEEDING OUT

In this book, I have attempted to show via example how I do the work of magic that actually looks like magic. However, the obviously sorcerous bits are not all of the bits! I spoke earlier of four points:

Devotion in action is to focus (make primary or "first") on that which is the most important to you. Discretion in action is the ability and willingness to make intelligent decisions. Integrity in action means doing what you say you will do, and doing it to the best of your ability. Consistency in action means you do all of these things all of the time.

These points are as much about, and our success depends as much upon, what we do not do as what we do instead.

You need to know and decide what is OK for you and what is not. These are boundary questions. This also requires doing the work required to gain knowledge of the self-hater, self-doubt, and delusion.

I've not met anyone who wouldn't be served by some kind of inner clean-up work. I was in therapy as a teen and didn't care for it, but I do think it helped some.

The single most useful magical tool I have found in the past decade is the Feeding Your Demons practice taught by Tsultrim Allione in her book of the same name. I tend to cycle into that work once a year for a few weeks at a time and it's a massive help. The practice is simple to learn, fascinating enough to keep me doing it, and the benefits are enormous. While I strongly suggest reading the book, the practice is basically this: Set up two seats for meditation, facing each other. Decide on the demon you wish to work with. In this practice, "demon" means problem, difficulty, or blockage, perhaps anxiety, fear, or something else that drains you or hinders you. Locate where you feel the demon residing in your body and then externalize the demon. This is what the second seat is for. The process then involves switching seats, being "yourself" and being "the demon" in turn, to find out what it's needs and desires are. You then then feed it the feeling resulting from the satisfaction of it's needs, and integrate it. It's amazingly effective.

Meditation is a huge help, and some form of it really should be practiced. You will need the quiet time to see what loops your mind is running. There is no such thing as being "bad" at meditation, though it sure seems like it some days! Since the "goal" is to simply sit and try to still the discursive mind by noticing its chatter and looping...well, if all you get is chatter and looping, that's OK. At least you will be one of the people who is aware of it, which is itself a source of great power.

Watch the looping of the discursive mind. These loops tend to be of the "nonsense and distraction" kind on one hand, and the "self-hater or self-abuse" (and not the fun kind!) on the other.

Deep relaxation is huge. If you perform the trance inductions and get very relaxed regularly, it will have already paid great dividends. We are beings designed to live in a generally low-stress environment with short bursts of acute stress, which tend to have a hormetic[1] effect. Instead, we mostly live in chronic stress states which are debilitating. Relaxation techniques are critical self-care in the modern environment. Any traveling, visions, etc., that may come are great and may certainly be helpful, but the time spent in the trance state is in itself golden.

Cleaning up your personal, mundane act is also a big deal. What do you do that you honestly don't want to be doing? Not because it's hard, but because it's shitty, either to yourself or to those around you. Make the decision to stop being shitty! This, while easier said than done, is absolutely doable. Make a list (and don't use this as another excuse to trash yourself) of the things that you won't do anymore. Make a list of the things you will do instead. Seek the better result. Expect that you will be successful. Know that you will fuck up. Just keep at it. Incremental improvements lead to radical change.

Clarify what is truly important to you. Some people place fame high

---

1   Hormetic stress is basically intense, irregular (acute) stress that produces a positive adaptation. Things like weight training, cold exposure, and the like are hormetic stresses. These are the "that which does not kill me makes me stronger" kind of things. The chronic stress many of us suffer is more of the "what does not kill me today will grind me down and kill me later" variety.

on the list, some a nice house. Some a family, some travel. Some prioritize service to others and some, sex with strangers. Take these things into your other practices. Take them into meditation, to your divination. See if you can find their core. See if you can find what blocks you. Take them into the Feeding Your Demons practice.

Clarify what is truly unimportant to you. What avenues of life hold no interest. Minimize your involvement there. The caveat being that unimportant isn't the same as difficult or boring. Lots of valuable things are difficult and boring.

Commit to practice. Practice, which is careful repetition with the intention to improve over time, is the key to most things. If I can practice treating my kids or coworkers more kindly, my relationship with them will change. There is no guarantee it will ever be perfect, but I can move it in a better direction. Likewise, if I commit to a practice of magic I will gain skill at it and understanding of it, at least "it" as it relates to me.

A committed magical practice can be a small thing. If you light a candle and make offerings to your helper spirits on a regular basis you will change things. You will deepen your connection to the Field. If you also add in a regular use of the Re/Claiming rite, you will find yourself at even greater ease, with more of your personal power available to you. If you add in something like the Six Ways ritual you will find you can navigate your life more effectively.

A committed relationship with your Gods if you are of that bent is also a practice. As is the regular reading of cards or other divination. We are what we do, and we get good at what we strive to be good at unless we are deceiving ourselves or are subject to other blockages.

Cleaning up the mess of your physical life helps. Getting your finances in order, even if they still aren't what you would like them to be, allows you to actually see what is going on in that sphere. Which allows intelligent action via magical or mundane means. Cleaning up your physical space is much the same. Even if you are unwilling to go deep minimalist, applying many of the concepts in Marie Kondo's book *The Life-Changing Magic of Tidying Up* should allow most people to purge a shit-ton of physical baggage. Her approach is decidedly magical and can be used for far more than cleaning house. KonMari (as she prefers to be called) also has a very interesting animist take on the world, and I consider this a very useful book from a magical perspective.

Be smart about where you place your energy. Again, take these ideas to the pendulum or cards. Take them into meditation. Sit with "where do I place my energy?" as a question in meditation or trance. If the answer doesn't suit you, make a different choice.

Know that the discursive, looping mind and the self-hater always seek to prolong delusion, always seek to perpetuate the loops. Far more than other people, these parts of self keep us where we would, if we were able to be clear and honest, rather not be. They can be tamed, but not eliminated, from all that I have seen.

In working to get a handle on the self-hater, I came up with my standard response to it a long time ago. It would pop up and say "You can't do that! That's not you! You'll fail and look stupid! People will mock you! Pity you!" As I learned to notice these shitty loops for what they were, I would respond to them (not indulge them!) by saying "but you are boring and entirely ruled by fear. I am not. I will do what seems good to me." There is no need and no benefit to arguing with these parts of self: they have no ability to be other than they are. Just firmly disregard their fearful little lies, and do whatever you can to turn down the volume on their whining.

We "tame" these shitty loops and voices by understanding them to be noise, not of actual value, and thus not worthy of continued attention. They are gifts to us of culture and upbringing for the most part, and like the hideous sweater your father or grandmother gave you, the hideous lies of the self-hater may well have come from the same source.

We tame them not by elimination, as they will always arise when we are tired, or scared. They at best go dormant. We tame them by turning up the signal on what we want, what we truly aspire to, via as many levels of word and deed as we can, magical or mundane. We tame them by turning down the volume on their unhelpful monologues, until their voices are like nothing but the sighing of the wind through leaves in the distance.

Clarity of purpose, clarity of questions, carefully choosing the currents that lead us forward are all ways to boost the signal. When we can say "I am here, and I am doing this, and I am going there" clearly, consistently, and back that up on both the magical and mundane levels, there is little for these loops and voices to attach to.

CHAPTER THIRTY

THE SHIP IN PRACTICE

As mentioned before, I like to think of our magic as a ship.

The Field is the sea, the currents, the wind, the sky, the stars, as well as all the birds, clouds, rain, and sea life. It is also at the deepest level the ship itself (as it is the root of everything perceivable) and ourselves. Over time, with consistent effort and clear focus, we build our ship plank by plank. We learn to read the patterns of the waves and currents and we draw to us a trusted crew of friends and allies.

The altar, which is any place where we gather to do our work, is like the wheel that steers the vessel, the rudder, the sails, the engine, as well as the instruments we use to navigate and adjust our course. We and our allied spirits man the sails and when needed, the oars. Divination, visions, and dreams are like the sailor up in the crow's nest with a spyglass keeping an eye out for obstacles and land, divining by the flight of birds, the songs of the sirens, and the witch-lights that shine deep in the waters at night.

The offerings, candles, incense, sigils and spells are both fuel and another type of general steering.

The point of all that imagery is that we should view what we do as a whole. We may well do discrete bits of work, but we must understand that we are a vessel with purpose, crew, and need of maintenance and care. In most cases, we will be the most effective and powerful when all aspects of our work function synergistically towards our goal.

Here is an example where the goal is to improve a financial scenario. Start by doing those things on the material side to improve the finances. See where you are "leaking" money, and stop it. Begin to get control of both spending and debt. Not only are these changes good and necessary, they actually add fuel to the magical fires you are starting.

You will also want to work the magical side. I suggest starting by running anything at all related to finances, job, savings, prosperity, and related issues that you can through the process taught in Tsultrim Allione's book *Feeding Your Demons*.[1] Then take to your altar.

At the altar, put on your fancy wizard hat, and do some of the following:

Do a Road Opening ritual for the Money Roads to clear obstacles.[2]

Do (or have someone do) some divination to see where you are blocked in relation to your financial world.

Make a petition for what you need financially.

Use that petition as the basis for a sugar or honey jar.

Make a money drawing box-vessel for the whole shebang, that your jar can sit on top of or inside of.

Begin compiling intentions for a shoal of sigils to work on the more discrete pieces of work. Perhaps a sigil for gaining the skills needed for a different, more lucrative kind of work. Another sigil for the clearing of debts. Another for a clear understanding of where you "bleed" money unintentionally, and another to call helper spirits to you that will help in drawing money to you. Create all these sigils, whatever makes sense in your specific case, and charge them. These then go into the vessel or the jar.

Start this work on the first sliver of the New Moon and push through to the Full.

Make offerings (water, food, candles, incense) to your Spirits, perhaps using a format like this:

Spirits and Powers who aid and guard me, please accept these offerings I give. May they nourish you and fulfill you, and may there

---

1 I think this book should be given to literally everyone, but especially those who would practice magic. It is a wildly effective method for mitigating or outright resolving a ton of issues that can block us or lead to delusion.

2 In Chapter Three I give two brief examples of Road Opening, using invocation and evocation. I suggest you develop a simple, brief rite for Open Roads, as they are about the most basic of truly useful workings. They don't need to be anything fancy, but they have a place in most types of work. Unless, of course, you are closing roads instead!

be peace between us for all of our days. Spirits who stand between me and prosperity, those who block the flow of money into my house, please accept these offerings I give. May you be nourished and fulfilled, and may there be peace between us for all of our days. I ask that you accept these offerings, and remove the blockages you have set that hinder the flow of money and prosperity into my house and life.

Then move onto asking for what you desire. Something like this. I do this while touching the sugar jar or the box that houses the shoal of sigils.

Powers and Spirits of Prosperity, come into this place. Slip inside this house as you pass by,[3] and bless it with your presence. Open the doors for wealth to flow to me. I am working to acquire a better job that brings in more money and gives me better health insurance. It would be awesome if I really liked it. Please guide me to what I can do to help myself in acquiring this employment. Keep me from straying down roads that are unhelpful. Bless me and my home with Prosperity. May there be peace between us always.

This is not a singular piece of work. This is many small pieces in what will be an ongoing practice, perhaps for weeks, perhaps for years. You build the ship, and then steer and change course as desired.

3 *Slip Inside This House,* The 13th Floor Elevators, *Easter Everywhere.*

CHAPTER THIRTY ONE

STAY CLEAN

In a larger way than in the rest of our lives, magic gives back what you put into it. Do your work with utmost honesty, and you will generally get good results. But magic is power, and all power can be dangerous. As Billy Idol says, there is nothing safe in this world.[1] That said, if you come into magic and face straight fucking forward,[2] you will generally do well. But this total responsibility thing is no joke. Say what you mean, do what you say, and as the song goes, one thing leads to another.[3]

However, as we muck about in our daily lives, sorcerous or not, we can (and often do) acquire a layer of dust, dirt, and grime. The sticker on our shoe is not a serious issue, but the riders stuck to our psychic selves can cause major problems.

Doing calming, centering, and grounding work helps quite a lot. Doing a regular practice of calling out to or calling down the powers you work with does as well. Regular use of the Stars of the Six Ways ritual will do more. Inner alchemical work (the orbits and vowel toning) does yet more. Offering work, more again, particularly if you make offerings those that would normally be inclined to hinder you.

Overall you are seeking to create a healthy, fertile magical ecosystem where all of the good, helpful powers are keeping the system humming along in a friendly and balanced manner. All of the above practices aid this. But just like in the physical body, sometimes we acquire a virus or bacterial infection. People also do engage in intentionally harmful magic, many of whom are on some level unaware of what they are doing. Whatever the cause, the end result is we can become psychically ill and weighted down.

There are a number of ways to work to keep this from happening and

---

1   *White Wedding*, Billy Idol.
2   Thanks to Fabeku Fatunmise for "face fucking forward."
3   *One Thing Leads to Another*, The Fixx.

to clear it up when it does. I will just look at a few and suggest that anyone working magic should own a copy of *Spiritual Cleansing* by Draja Mikaharic and Jason Miller's *Protection and Reversal Magic* for when things get out of whack, as it is very likely they will at some point.

Salt is your friend. If you live by the ocean, getting in it periodically is a good idea (unless you have reasons not to). Otherwise, salt added to a bath is good. Washing your hands with salt and water can often clear things up quite a bit.

The classic purifying herbs are Rue and Hyssop. Rosemary is also a good choice that is readily available. Making a tea of any of those three (remembering to consecrate) and adding them to a bath will do wonders. This can be done without a bathtub, just take your tea, add it to a good size basin of water, and wash with it, giving particular attention to the hands, feet, and head.

When this is not enough, add a spoonful of vinegar to the water. This is viewed as a harsh method and can be too effective, removing positive influences as well as the negatives. Afterwards, especially if you use vinegar, consecrate yourself. The Re/Claiming rite will do this very well.

In all cases, at every step where it makes sense, consecrate! Ask the component bits to help you. *"As is your nature, I ask you to cleanse me of all impurities, all harmful energies, and to leave me clean."*

Regular spiritual bathing is a good idea. Once a week should generally do the trick, but there may be times where you find you need to do it every day.

The Lord's Prayer and Psalm 23 can be useful to those who are comfortable with them, as are many other "known" prayers.

ARCHANGEL MICHAEL

I am not a follower of any religion. I was raised with the tiniest of exposure to the church in my earliest years, but that was it. This has not stopped me from working with Archangel Michael.

The spirit-story is that Michael is balance to, and nearly twin brother to Lucifer. Both can be helpful spirits, Lucifer on the illumination end of things and Michael on the protective side of things. Both are very old spirits, and well predate any written record we have of them. Part of their power and usefulness has to do with this factor of age.[4] How they were mythologized in the Abrahamic religions is another thing entirely.

To work with Michael in this capacity, acquire or create an image of Michael of any kind. This can be one of the Catholic cards or medals, a copy of his Angelic seal, or some other appropriate symbol. Included is the design of a talisman I made for him that he seems to like. He's generally a very willing spirit.

FOR ARCHANGEL MICHAEL

Pick one day a week, Sunday is good but consistency is more important than which day. On that day, offer cool water and perhaps flowers if you are into that kind of thing, and offer incense. You can dress a candle for him, and then ask him for his help. This is a text that I have had good results with both for myself and with clients.

---

4   Heretical theological nonsense is often very useful in sorcery.

By the Stars in the East and the Stars in the West
By the Stars in the North and the Stars in the South
By the Stars Above and the Stars Below
Michael, Archangel, Flaming Sword, Divine Messenger
Come to me, Aid me, Guard me
Cover me with your wings
Protect me with your flaming sword
Wrap me in your fury at evil
Repel all that would harm me & mine
Drive them from me
Drive them from this place
Drive them from this time
Burn them with the light of the Maker
Burn them with the Fire from Heaven
Come unto me, Michael Archangel
Aid and guard me in this work
Aid and guard me in the here and now
Aid and guard me in the past and future
As it was, as it is, and as it shall be
Flaming Sword, Fire from Heaven
Be with me now & always
As it was, as it is, as it shall be.

In time this type of work will develop a solid bond between you and Michael. The general framework is also valid for many Others you might wish to work with.

SAFETY

I've done a good deal of damage to myself by falling down (something I have a major talent for). I have scars on my forehead from walking into door frames. Yes, plural on both counts. People hurt themselves, their loved ones, strangers, and pretty much wreck their lives doing literally anything and everything. Eating. Drinking. Walking. Driving. Aspirating toys. Making love. Falling through plate glass windows. Sneezing. The list is actually endless.

There are risks in doing magic, same as there are in eating a meal. There is a potential for doing yourself lasting harm, just like getting behind the wheel of a car.

Let me clarify here. If sorcery works, and it does, then it can work for or against us. If we can call good things into our lives, we can call bad things as well. If we can forge attachments (in a positive sense) to friendly spirits that wish to help us, we can also forge negative attachments with spirits that wish to harm us. We can use the tools of magic to cut through the delusions that chain us into unhelpful patterns or we can use them to reinforce the delusions that keep us chained. I've known practitioners who used magic to survive rather serious psychological disorders, and those whose practices made their lives much worse. These are not strictly psychological issues, although they most commonly first manifest as such. I've been outright attacked by Others who wanted me out of my body so they could use it. Not even joking. I've exorcised spirits that were preying on the physical and psychic vitality of the weak. I've been involved in workings that created straight up water pouring out of the telephone Poltergeist-type side effects, and I once knew a whole working group who developed weird ass nasty skin conditions from the gods know where. It really is important that we do the work to stay clean, stay clear, and stay functional. Forge strong alliances with helpful Others (like the Archangels), and be wary with entities that strike you as hungry or malevolent. Make no agreements that don't sit 100% right with you. You can always say "no." The approach I use has been developed to mitigate as many of these issues as possible, but there is no way to do this work entirely without hazards. Know that they are real, and take care of your shit. This is not said here to scare you off, but to hopefully instill a bit of what the tactical world calls situational awareness. Situational awareness is basically "paying attention to what is going on around you" so that you can react accordingly. A run of bad luck, random ill health, and the like may be no more than they seem, but for the practicing magician the response really needs to occur on both the mundane and magical levels at the same time. That said, if you approach the work intelligently and are proactive on the spiritual cleansing work, for the most part, things will generally work out well.

An idea I find helpful to remaining spiritually clear is the concept of "luminous fibers," which comes to us via Carlos Castaneda.

The luminous fibers are a form of psychic, tentacle-like structures that extend from the body. When we enter into contact with people, our fibers can get stuck to each other. Maybe you have experienced those people who kind of "slime you" in a brief moment of meeting, where it is hard to get "them" off of you? Luminous fibers hard at work!

Now I don't actually go in for the whole, epic recapitulation process that is taught by some who follow Castaneda's work (which is not to say it is without value or does not work; it's just not what I do), but I like the concept of the luminous fibers. It remains the best description I've found of the phenomena, and as a story it is "true enough" to work with.

Part of the process of spiritual cleansing is to remove these fibers, these attachments, that cling to us and link us to unhelpful people and energies. I scan for these attachments and remove them, a bit like picking lint from a shirt I am wearing, using a process I call scraping.

Scraping is a good way to shed the luminous fibers and other unhelpful attachments that may cling to us. It is easier to explain by having you stand up (if you are sitting) and actually do something first.

So stand up, and run your left hand all over your body, everywhere you can easily reach, as if you were wiping away a layer of water from your skin. Now do the same with your right hand, everywhere you can reach easily with that hand. Run your hands one at a time all over your body, head, arms, legs, feet, hands. This should only take about thirty seconds or a minute. That is the practice run! Now go and find yourself an iron (or steel) tool. This can be a dull knife (seriously dull, you could lose an ear if it's sharp!) or even a screwdriver.

Now repeat what you just did, "scraping" an inch or so above your body, arms, head, legs, feet, and hands with your tool while saying out loud: *"I scrape myself clean of the luminous fibers and unhelpful attachments that cling to me, leaving myself clean, clear, and whole."* Scrape as much of your body as you can without major contortions, and you will likely sense a change of state. If you do not sense this "clean and clear" state the first time (or even the fiftieth!) don't worry, just know that what you are doing is having the desired effect, and in time you will likely actually feel the difference. This is an excellent daily practice, one that I tend to use right before I do the Re/Claiming rite.

There is a classical magical idea that is relevant here, and that is contagion. Contagion deals with the idea that once two things have been in close proximity or touching, they continue to affect one another. Contagion can be worked with via things like the use of someone else's hair or an article of their clothing to work magic for (or on) them, or even the use of their footprints.

Of more interest to me is the idea of contagion of ideas, thought processes, and conceptions of limitation and possibility acquired via close contact with others. Like the luminous fibers, these things are sticky. They can influence our perceptions without us being fully aware of them. They are contagions like a virus is.

Take some time in meditation or trance to ask where contagion plays out in your life. Are you constantly down at work? At school or at a friend's house? Around certain people? Is this feeling originating in you, or are you picking it up from others? I've known people who scream "psychic vampirism!" at the merest hint of this kind of thing. There is a piece of truth in that. Like inviting a vampire into our home, often we give tacit approval for this kind of contact and so the luminous fibers or other kinds of contagions from others can attach to us easily.

If you determine this is the case, here is something you can try. Do this work before you enter the problem space or are going to be around the problem person. Begin by doing your general cleansing, using ritual, bathing, talismans, until you feel light and clear. Scrape away the fibers. Consecrate yourself using the Re/Claiming rite or whichever method you prefer. Use an oil of some sort, whatever you fancy,[5] and anoint your hands, feet, and head to "seal" the consecration.[6] When you enter the place, or into proximity of the person that causes you difficulties, consciously, either under your breath or internally, deny them or it the right of influence. *"I refuse to be touched by you, to provide energy to you, or be unduly influenced by you without my explicit statement of consent."* Repeat this part

---

5   You can use scented oils or specifically magical oils of course, but simple olive oil is a fine all-purpose oil. I am with Draja Mikaharic that mineral oil is in most cases a no-go!

6   You know the drill by now. Tell the component parts what you are doing and/or what you want them to do. "Creature of oil, I call on you to aid and guard me and to seal this consecration so that none can do me harm."

as necessary. If things get wonky, run the three orbits (I've excused myself for a moment and run the orbits or done the "Stars of the Six Ways" rite in the bathroom on more than one occasion) to get yourself centered and energized. Be consistent!

Expect some flak. I've been in rooms where I knocked over my cup, dropped books or pens, etc., for a solid ten minutes, well beyond the level of absurdity before things calmed down. People are stranger in their response than many spirits, and it is often harder to predict their reactions to this kind of work. The person who normally drags you down will likely respond poorly if they don't get the contact and acceptance that they are used to. They can get whiny, angry, accusatory, very hands-on-touchy (this is especially odd if your relationship does not usually involve contact), or get very spaced out and confused. Be gentle but firm.[7]

I've seen this process shed friends very rapidly on occasion. Sometimes this really is a case of (usually unintentional) psychic vampirism, and they will now have to go elsewhere to find what they need to feed on energetically. But more often it is lighter, a form of codependence that falls apart when you refuse to allow it anymore. I've only had one instance where it made sense to actually talk to the other person about it. They came to me and asked what had changed and if I had changed it. I told them, and they were fairly cool about it. They asked what they could do on their end to "fix" things, and in the end, we remained friends. More often it is a relationship killer, for better or worse.

---

7   Please, please, please use your intelligence and discretion when dealing with people or situations that might get violent. This is no joke. In situations where violence is already the norm, this process can be a trigger.

CHAPTER THIRTY TWO

RETICULATION

When I was a child I knew an older boy who had a sixteen-foot reticulated python. This was about the coolest thing ever! I have ever since loved the word "reticulated."

In time I learned that reticulated meant "net like structure."

So reticulate means to form or move via a net or network like structure.

The sorcerous world is a reticular one. Built of threads or strands of connection, of contagion, vectors of change and manifestation. Like a spider's web, a touch on one thread sends information throughout the entire creation.

This magical net is expansive. It spreads a long, long way beyond us. It is helpful to think of ourselves not as wielding the net like a fisherman, but more like existing as a node or knot on a vast, Field-wide network or web.

The altar, working space, even our magical selves are in themselves nodes on this vast net. Our works send out ripples through this reticulate structure. The work we do, rituals, sigils, meditation, and spells all send out information to and through the web.

If we make the songs we sing (the works we do) clear enough and enticing enough we can call to us connections from nodes farther afield.

It helps to consider that in a practical sense the nodes on the net are not fixed points, not hard-set locations. This is where being able to use our sense of the material world can shift from being helpful to being unhelpful if we get caught in viewing our metaphors as concrete.

If we can accept that these nodes move and shift proximity due to similarity of purpose and intention, this opens us to the idea that as we work on the web, we draw to us things that have affinity with us and support what we do. So effectively the other interested nodes come to have stronger bonds and closer connections with us. It is "as if" they have moved closer together on the web. This can be decidedly helpful, or decidedly unhelpful!

This is helpful if we are working clearly and what I think of as cleanly.

This is not about moral purity, this type of clean, but more about a clean signal. A clean signal is largely free of undesired noise, and so transmits itself clearly. If you have ever played a guitar, this is much like fretting a note. When you pick up a guitar for the first time and fret a note it doesn't usually work all that well. You don't have the strength, callouses or skills to fret the note firmly and cleanly so when you pluck the string, it tends to make weird buzzes and other noise. As you gain skill and strength through practice, you learn to play clean, clear, articulate notes. If you try to play a guitar that is in bad shape or set up poorly, you may still get all sorts of noise.

In the audio recording world, they talk about signal to noise ratio. In our guitar example, if I play a clean, clear note, and there is no unwanted sound whatsoever on the recording, I have a clear signal, a very high signal to noise ratio. If instead the note is not clear, and there is a lot of unwanted background noise in the recording, I have a poor signal to noise ratio.

By working cleanly and clearly, we improve the signal to noise ratio. In other words, the signals, messages, and calls we send out on the strands of the web are transmitted clearly. When we intend to send out an A minor, what is received out in the wider web is an A minor. When we ask a question about our work, we are likely to get responses based on our question or signal, not the noise (which can either obscure our message or contain unintended messages in itself) that we have sent out along with it.

This clear messaging helps draw to us clear responses. It also helps grow connections between our node and other nodes that have similar interests and approaches. In practice, this brings us and them closer together, and our little section of the web becomes tuned in a particular way. This locates us in a kind of affinity group and is a fine example of symbiosis.

We could now take this image a bit further and say that spirits, be they incarnate or not, are nodes on the web. If we consistently work clearly with our spirits, saints, servitors, and deities, we in a sense draw ourselves into a functionally closer group that has stronger, clearer bonds.

This closer group can be said to have resonance. This resonance suggests that when I send out a clear signal (by magical work, meditation, or other means) or ask clear questions (in trance or divination) the other nodes in my group pick up and repeat or otherwise amplify my signal.

This amplification means my signal can travel farther out along the web, and contact and attract still other nodes and perhaps draw them into our affinity group, which produces yet greater resonance, and extends and strengthens the entire process.

Remembering that this process is always happening, it is important to also recall that it isn't always for the better. If we are a mess, unclear, always distracted, angry, or delusional, the entire system reinforces this state. We draw nodes together that have affinity to this mess, and which will then work to support and boost its signal. It can and does get ugly!

It seems to me that most of the problems, troubles, and failures perceived by many practitioners of the magical and sacred arts can also be explained using this net model.

Some of what goes on in magical practice seems to me more like another kind of net, a fishing net. This makes some sense on the surface, as with a net we can catch a lot of fish. It's an effective tool. However, we can also catch things we don't want to in our net, like when we try to scoop up some tuna and we end up with a mako shark in our boat! Fishing with a net can be interesting and exciting, but it can also piss off those who get caught in it. Unless you are dealing with a serious problem, capturing spirits and holding them via threat or force leads to very irritated entities.

Those who choose to use the net to fish, tend to end up with sharks on deck at some point. It's just sort of a given, and those who prefer this approach either get good at dealing with sharks, get bit, or both.

Those who work to build and strengthen a web of affinities, more like a neural net, and do the work to be a strong and clear node, attract other strong and clear nodes. I obviously suggest the web-and-node approach pretty much exclusively.

One benefit of working with the web-and-node approach is that our cluster of nodes becomes less attractive to hostile presences to mess with. Spirits are not stupid and don't tend to poke a stick (unlike people) into a whole section of the web that will respond strongly in a unified fashion against the intrusion. From this perspective, the web-and-node approach builds systemic immunity. We might still get a bit ill from time to time, but we are more likely to recover quickly and will more easily restore equilibrium.

It could be correctly said that I have told versions of this story repeatedly in this book, and I have. It could also be said that this is the subtext of the entire book, and it is. It is in my experience perhaps the most important and most often neglected aspect of the practice of magic and sorcery.

CHAPTER THIRTY THREE

DIRT SORCERY

I keep a box of finely sifted and heat-treated dirt from rabbit warrens on my altar, as a connection to creatures who actually live in the underworld, and I use it for dirt sorcery.

I borrowed the dirt-box idea from geomancy, which is a form of divination. Mine is a wooden cigar box, filled with dirt from the entrances of jackrabbit and cottontail burrows. I collected the soil from warrens all around my house. I sifted it to remove all but the finest soils (and get rid of the cactus spines!) and then sterilized it in an oven set to 180 degrees for a few hours. This was to kill any rodent-born nastiness.

My plan was to use the box, representing and actually made of the land around me, to draw sigils in. I do use it this way, but more often I use it in the way I describe next.

For particular workings, I find my eyes straying to this box. At those times I will open it up, and enter into trance. I bring to mind whatever my intention is, and when I have it very strongly present, I begin to sink my fingers into the dirt. I let my fingers make patterns, with no concern for artistry or logic. I stop when I feel done, when the magic has merged with the dirt. Then I pinch out a bit of the soil and use it to dress candles or petitions or to add to a vessel or charm bag.

I have many ideas about this practice, and why it works so well, mainly having to do with links to the actual land I dwell upon and the wild fertility of bunnies. The important thing, however, is that it works. I expect it would work even with soils not so strongly linked to the rabbit folk, but you'll have to try it to find out.

As for dirt sorcery itself, it is a term I coined years ago to describe my own practice. Originally I would tell people, when they asked for my thoughts about some arcane system of magic in which I had no interest, "I'm just a rocks and string kind of guy." This usually stopped these lines of inquiry, and it was actually true. In time I started to call it dirt sorcery, and rocks and string remain important parts of my practice!

It is my belief that magic is "just" something we humans do. That for the past few hundred years some of us in the West have forgotten this doesn't seem incredibly relevant when considered on the scale of human time and history. Those of us who have stepped away from the magical world did so only relative moments ago, and that world is still embedded in us (as children of the Field) far too deeply for us to stay away for long. Magic is in our blood, bones and breath.

Every act of magic has its roots deep in the past, a lineage of actions built on a similar understanding of the worlds we inhabit. Like affects like, which gets named "the law of similarity." Things once in contact remain linked, "the law of contagion." Magic to contact and seek aid from Aerial or Stellar spirits becomes Angelic Magic and that to work with or compel the Chthonic or Terrestrial spirits becomes Demonic Magic.

All of these theories and concepts are born in the bodily knowledge of all of us children of the soil. First from Africa and then outwards as we spread through the ages into Oceania, Asia, Europe, and the Americas. We may be told that we are wiser, better, and somehow "more" than those who came before us (or those blessed ones who still fully inhabit a magical world), but from dirt we came, in dirt we grub (or pay or force someone else to do so on our behalf) for our survival, and our spiritual and psychical realities are all experienced via these bodies of ours, born of the dirt.

Since I do not really believe in the myth of progress and its "always upwards, always better" story, I choose the older tales. We are all born of the soil, the sea, the rain, the sun. We are born of a great cow, a great serpent, a tree. All of these seem like more truthful tales.

So my altar is filled with the remains of noble creatures, goat and wildcat and coyote, raven, crow, owl, and the spurs from particularly good roosters I have known. These are reminders of who my compatriots are on this sphere. They all have likely known more than I, and all have likely been more honest. At the least more honestly themselves, as it seems their people are less willfully cruel to one another, and so they seem to be less cruelly shaped by their societies.

I find comfort in all of this: this is all knowledge that begets freedom. We are born of people, some good, some bad. We share genetic markers with a few of them. Our family line stretches back more than a million years, and I at least assume those were some pretty sharp folks for me to be able to sit here now, writing this book.

My family of fifty or three hundred thousand years ago looked different that it does now. They were definitely tougher that I am! And they knew in a deeper fashion, I believe, all of these things I am writing about in this text. Different times meant different names, tools, methods. But what was in them is in me, is in all of us. We are as trees born from trees born from trees, all risen up from deep and ancient roots. That's a whole lot of connection, spanning a vast amount of time.

I do not believe we can reconstruct anything accurately. Context being king, what my many-thousand-year-old cousins knew is forever lost to me. Their whole world is lost to me. But my roots still reach back to and tap the same source. They still nourish me from those vanished depths if I allow it. I invite you to allow it as well. I invite you to consider this view of ourselves as inherently magical, as inherently connected to the earth and the Field, as inherently able to thrive on a psychic level even as our world makes it harder in many ways to survive physically or emotionally.

I do not believe my approach is for everyone, is the right way, or any such nonsense. But I do think it can serve as a bridge of sorts. A bridge of mist, of bone, blood, of spirit and soil to span a gap that is, as all gaps are, essentially empty. A modern bridge of concrete and steel cannot take us where we would like to and perhaps need to go. I'll take the dirt road, the spirit road, with the coyotes and the ravens, as my people always have.

Aidan Wachter
August 21, 2017
New Mexico

SUGGESTED READING

While I have attempted to provide a largely stand-alone text, the following five books will create a very workable library of practical magic that covers a lot of bases without being exhaustive in any way, with an emphasis of keeping your selves, mind, and environment fully functional.

Allione, Tsultrim, *Feeding Your Demons: Ancient Wisdom for Resolving Inner Conflict* (Little, Brown and Company, 2008)

Fries, Jan, *Visual Magick: A Manual of Freestyle Shamanism* (Mandrake of Oxford 1992)

Mickaharic, Draja, *Spiritual Cleansing: A Handbook of Psychic Protection* (Weiser Books, 2012)

Miller, Jason, *Protection and Reversal Magick* (New Page Books, 2006)

Yronwode, Catherine, *Hoodoo Herb and Root Magic: A Materia Magica of African-American Conjure* (Lucky Mojo Curio Company, 2002)

This next set of titles will further extend this knowledge base, while going much deeper in ways that may be quite beneficial:

Dukes, Ramsey, *The Little Book of Demons: The Positive Advantages of the Personification of Life's Problems* (Aeon Books, 2005)

Dukes, Ramsey, *How To See Fairies: Discover Your Psychic Powers in Six Weeks* (Aeon Books, 2011)

Elias, Camelia, *Marseille Tarot: Towards the Art of Reading* (Eyecorner Press, 2014)

Elias, Camelia, *The Oracle Travels Light: Principles of Magic with Cards* (Eyecorner Press, 2015)

Fries, Jan, *Seidways: Shaking, Swaying and Serpent Mysteries* (Mandrake of Oxford, 2009)

Kondo, Marie, *The Life-Changing Magic of Tidying Up: The Japanese Art of Decluttering and Organizing* (Ten Speed Press, 2014)

Mickaharic, Draja, *A Century of Spells* (Samuel Weiser, 1985)

Miller, Jason, *The Sorceror's Secrets: Strategies in Practical Magick* (New Page Books, 2009)

Nhat Hahn, Thich, *The Heart of the Buddha's Teaching: Transforming Suffering into Peace, Joy, and Liberation* (Harmony, 2015)

Nhat Hahn, Thich, *Understanding Our Mind: 50 Verses on Buddhist Psychology* (Parallax Press, 2002)

Rätsch, Christian, Müller-Ebeling, Claudia, Storl, Wolf-Dieter, *Witchcraft Medicine: Healing Arts, Shamanic Practices, and Forbidden Plants* (Inner Traditions, 2003)

Snell, Lionel, *My Years of Magical Thinking* (The Mouse That Spins, 2017)

White, Gordon, *The Chaos Protocols: Magical Techniques for Navigating the New Economic Reality* (Llewellyn Publications, 2016)

My magical roots are in chaos magic and related approaches to sorcery largely influenced and inspired by Austin Osman Spare. While not all of these books fall directly into that camp, they are all lasting influences. Not so much recommended as deserving of a place of honor at the table:

Carroll, Peter J., *Liber Null & Psychonaut: An Introduction to Chaos Magic* (Weiser Books, 1987)

Chumbley, Andrew D., *Azoetia* (Xoanon, 1992)

Dukes, Ramsey, SSOTBME *Revised – An Essay on Magic* (The Mouse That Spins, 2002)

Grant, Kenneth, *Images & Oracles of Austin Osman Spare* (Fulgar Limited, 2003)

Hall, Nicholas, *Chaos & Sorcery* (Joh. Bohmeier Verlag, 1998)

Mace, Stephen, *Stealing the Fire from Heaven* (Dagon Productions, 2003)

Sherwin, Ray, *The Book of Results* (Lulu, 2005)

Sherwin, Ray, *Theatre of Magick* (self published, no date)

Spare, Austin Osman, *From the Inferno to Zos, The Writings and Images of Austin Osman Spare, Vol. 1* (First Impressions, 1993)

Thee Temple ov Psychick Youth, *Thee Grey Book* (T.O.P.Y., 1982)

And lastly, a few strays. Some deep history, and books otherwise mentioned in the text. The Eliade and Lecouteux are highly recommended, as is Gordon White's *Star.Ships*.

Burroughs, William S., *My Education, A Book of Dreams* (Penguin Books, 1996)

Carroll, Peter J., *Liber Kaos* (Weiser Books, 1992)

Eliade, Mircea, *The Sacred and The Profane: The Nature of Religion* (Harcourt Brace Jovanovich, 1987)

Eliade, Mircea, *Shamanism: Archaic Techniques of Ecstasy* (Princeton University Press, 2004)

Hoffman, Enid, *Huna: A Beginner's Guide* (Para Research, 1976)

Lecouteux, Claude, *Phantom Armies of the Night: The Wild Hunt and the Ghostly Processions of the Undead* (Inner Traditions, 2011)

Lecouteux, Claude, *The Return of the Dead: Ghosts, Ancestors, and the Transparent Veil of the Pagan Mind* (Inner Traditions, 2009)

Starhawk, *Truth or Dare: Encounters with Power, Authority, and Mystery* (HarperOne 1989)

White, Gordon, *Star.Ships* (Scarlet Imprint, 2016)

INDEX

CPSIA information can be obtained
at www.ICGtesting.com
Printed in the USA
BVHW03s2308160918
527342BV00004B/66/P